Witchcraft

THE HISTORY AND MYTHOLOGY

Witchcraft

THE HISTORY AND MYTHOLOGY

Richard Marshall

CRESCENT BOOKS
NEW YORK · AVENEL

Page 1: *A spinning witch, in a 16th century woodcut by Hans Holbein.*

Page 2: *Witches' Sabbath, by Francisco de Goya (1746–1828).*

Page 3: *Tituba and her young charges in Salem, Massachusetts.*

Right: *Faust, protected by his magic circle, meets Mephistopheles; illustration from an early edition of Christopher Marlowe's* Tragicall History of Dr. Faustus.

This 1995 edition published by Crescent Books, distributed by
Random House Value Publishing, Inc.
40 Engelhard Avenue
Avenel, New Jersey 07001

Random House
New York ★ Toronto ★ London ★ Sydney ★ Auckland

A *Saraband* book

Copyright © 1995 Saraband
Design © Ziga Design

A CIP catalog record for this book is available from the Library of Congress

ISBN 0-517-14083-7

10 9 8 7 6 5 4 3 2 1

Printed in China

This book is dedicated to Rebecca Lemp and all those others, mostly women, who were tortured and executed in the interests of bigotry and greed; and to all those, in various parts of the world, who still suffer from prejudice and intolerance.

Acknowledgement is gratefully made to reprint a passage from *Encyclopedia of Witchcraft and Demonology* by Rossell Hope Robbins. Copyright © 1959 by Crown Publishers, Inc. Reprinted by permission of Crown Publishers, Inc.

Contents

Introduction: The Devil Steps Out

Millions of spiritual creatures walk the Earth
Unseen, both when we wake, and when we sleep.
—John Milton, *Paradise Lost*, Book IV

On the morning of February 8, 1855, people in south Devonshire, western England, woke to a heavy snowfall. And to something else: for hundreds of miles, from Topsham to Teignmouth to Dawlish, something had left a line of hoof-marks in the snow. They went up walls and over roofs, and crossed the two-mile-wide estuary of the river Exe. Whatever made them had walked on two legs, with a stride of about eight inches.

There were explanations. The tracks had been made by a kangaroo. By a badger, a swan. Or perhaps by a toad, or a hare that kept its feet together as it hopped across roofs and over walls. There was another explanation too, and a strange story to go with it: hunters and hounds had followed the tracks into a wood, but the hounds turned tail, baying in terror, and the hunters followed them. The explanation—which most people found far more credible than the kangaroos and hoofed toads offered by the experts—was that the hoof-prints had been made by the Devil.

The events in south Devon that year weren't unique. On March 17 *The Illustrated London News* reported that similar tracks were found every year in the snow on a low hill in Poland, near the Galician border, and the locals thought they were caused by a "supernatural agency." In 1840, the London *Times* (March 14) had reported the finding of strange tracks over an area of some twelve miles in the Scottish mountains.

Opposite: The Garden of Earthly Delights *(1492; detail, center panel) by Hieronymus Bosch. Strange flowers and spiritual birds populate a version of unfallen Eden. Completed four years after the European witch-craze began, the painting has been interpreted as an exposition of the Adamite heresy, which celebrated everything primordial, including sexual freedom.*

Below: *Reclining satyr: Greece, 6th century BC; a version more polite than some of the horned and shaggy haunters of wild places, These disturbers of nymphs lurked unregenerate in European woods and fields till the early years of this century, ensuring harvests and inspiring dreams— the bold spirits of unreformed nature.*

They resembled those of a foal, but were longer, and to judge from their depth had been made by a creature of considerable weight. Perhaps (although the *Times* didn't suggest this) they were made by something of around the size of an ox. A Japanese archive (*Kokon Chomonshu*, quoted in *Notes and Queries*, 9-6.225) describes how "in the year 929 the Imperial Palace was found one morning full of demon's tracks as big as an ox's and coloured red and blue."

Cloven Hooves and Crones
Like the Devonshire fields on that cold morning in 1855, the byways and thoroughfares of history also bear the tracks of strange hoofed beings with two legs. For the Greeks, they were the shaggy-shanked sileni, half-human and half-goat, exaggeratedly phallic, devoted to sex and wine. They were the attendants of Dionysus, the god of many faces—of the vine and (in the form of Dionysus Zagreus) The Wild Hunt—who sometimes appeared in a black goat-skin, sometimes as a bull, and whose female followers were the ravening and immodest maenads, thought by their critics to be no better than "coursing bitches."

For the Greeks and Romans, the hoofed and horned god was Pan, a goat-legged lurker in the woods, a hard-drinker, pipe-player, seducer of nymphs and coupler with maenads. He was also a bestower of fertility on flocks, but capriciously—a word that comes from the Latin word for "goat." The same personage appears in the form of satyrs, fauns, and, among the Russians, as goat-legged woodland spirits called *ljeschies*.

From Pan's name we get the word used to describe an overturning of the ordinary or common senses, "panic," for all these goat-gods express instinct over reason, anarchy over order, ecstasy over asceticism, abundance over constraint. Concerned with the fertility of seed,

A WITCH AT WORK

When the Greek hero Jason returned to his homeland after capturing the Golden Fleece, his wife Medea, a formidable sorcerer, undertook to restore the youth and vigor of his aged father, Aeson. The following account of the operation was published in 1855 by the mythologist Thomas Bulfinch:

"The next full moon she issued forth alone while all creatures slept; not a breath stirred the foliage, and all was still; to the stars she addressed her incantations, and to the moon; and to Hecate, the goddess of the underworld, and to Tellus, the goddess of the earth, by whose power plants potent for enchantment are produced. She invoked the gods of the woods and caverns, of lakes and rivers, of winds and vapors. While she

spoke the stars shone brighter, and presently a chariot descended through the air, drawn by flying serpents. She ascended it, and borne aloft made her way to distant regions, where potent plants grew which she knew how to select for her purpose. Nine nights she employed in her search, and during that time came not within the doors of her palace nor under any roof, and shunned all intercourse with mortals.

She next erected two altars, the one to Hecate, the other to Hebe, the goddess of youth, and sacrificed a black sheep, pouring libations of milk and wine. She implored Pluto [Hades] and his stolen wife [Proserpine] that they would not hasten to take the old man's life. Then she directed that Aeson be led forth, and having thrown him into a deep sleep by a charm, had him laid on a bed of herbs, like one dead. Jason and all others were kept away from the place, that no profane eyes might look upon her

mysteries. Then, with streaming hair, she thrice moved around the altars, dipped flaming twigs in the blood, and laid them thereon to burn. Meanwhile the caldron with its contents was got ready. In it she put magic herbs, with seeds and flowers of acrid juice, stones from the distant east, and sand from the shore of the all-surrounding ocean; hoar frost, gathered by moonlight, a screech owl's head and wings, and the entrails of a wolf. She added fragments of the shells of tortoises, and the liver of stags—animals tenacious of life—and the head and beak of a crow, that outlives nine generations of

men. These and many other things 'without a name' she boiled together for her purposed work, stirring them up with a dry olive branch; and behold! The branch when taken out instantly became green, and before long was covered with leaves and a plentiful growth of young olives; and as the liquor boiled and bubbled, and sometimes ran over, the grass wherever the sprinklings fell shot forth with a verdure like that of spring.

Seeing that all was ready, Medea cut the throat of the old man and let out all his blood, and poured into his mouth and into his wound the juices of her caldron. A soon as he had completely imbibed them, his hair and beard laid by their whiteness and assumed the blackness of youth; his paleness and emaciation were gone; his veins were full of blood, his limbs of vigor and robustness. Aeson is amazed at himself, and remembers that such as he now is, he was in his youthful days forty years before."

Above: Hecate, by William Blake. The Queen of Witches, shown by the mystical Blake with spell-book, owl, monstrous bat, and grazing night-mare. She is comely, forceful, and mysteriously lit in some otherwise dark region of the painter's mind.

they are more concerned with the earth than with the sky; with the way of Dionysus, not the celestial way of Apollo the sun god.

A more purely subterranean figure was also concerned with the welfare of the seed, and this was Hecate, Goddess of the Dead, Queen of Witches, the most dreadful of all deities. She had the form of a hideous old woman, a crone with three heads—of a dog, a lion, and a horse—and hissing snakes hung from her shoulders. Those seeking magical powers made sacrifices of dogs, honey and black female lambs to her, possibly at some place where three roads met. Her most famous priestess was the witch Medea.

But Hecate was also the friend of Demeter, the goddess of fertility, and when Demeter's daughter Persephone (who was the guardian of the young Dionysus) was kidnapped by Hades and taken to the underworld, Hecate helped the distraught goddess to locate her. When Hades agreed to let Persephone return to the upper world for nine months every year, Hecate kept a watchful eye on her during the three months she had to spend in the underworld. The interpretation of this myth is as follows: Persephone's liberation from the underworld represents the growing season, her three months underground the period when the earth lies fallow; Demeter's two daughters, Core and Persephone,

crop-destroying hail. A person's health could be damaged by a witch, and the most powerful of them could cause death. Wealth and luck were subject to their powers, and in southern Europe some people are thought to possess this witch's ability in the form of the Evil Eye: even a glance from such a person can blight a crop or bring misfortune. Witches also sought the power of foreseeing the future, and with the Devil's help they obtained immunity to some kinds of pain, and were able to travel great distances in a short time. To achieve these ends witches cast spells, made magical images, pills, potions and powders, committed gross blasphemies, and were devoted to obscene and sometimes murderous rituals.

Although the word "witch" is gender-neutral (it derives from the Old English *wiccian*, meaning to bewitch, whence *wicca*, *wycca* or *wyche* for a male witch, *wicce*, *wycce*, *wicche* for a female witch), the witchfinder's work brought him

Left: *A dying man is visited by a devilish hobgoblin and visions from his past in this Victorian lantern slide.*

Below: *Witch with broomstick, riding a silly goose; a 19th-century fairy tale illustration, rendering those whom the church and state once burned quite fit for the nursery.*

with Hecate form a maiden-nymph-crone triad that represents three stages in the life of the corn: the unripe, the ripe and the harvested.

By the middle ages, the Devil himself, God's principal antagonist and the implacable enemy of mankind, had become (by an evolution described in chapter three) the cloven-hoofed figure we know today, and his supposed consorts, whether they were as vigorous as maenads, or like the crones cast in the mold of Hecate, were burned alive in their thousands.

Compacts with the Devil

In the narrow Judaeo-Christian definition of witchcraft that we owe to the prosecutors of the 15th, 16th and 17th centuries, a witch is a person who seeks to obtain supernatural powers by making a compact with the Devil or one of his demons, and who tries to use them for an evil purpose. Often the witch's target was the fertility of crops or animals, but she could also make a woman infertile, or a man impotent. By casting love spells, she could obtain romance and sexual compliance for herself or a client. Witches also sought power over the weather, producing droughts, storms and

Right: Two Witches
*by Hans Baldung
Grien, 1480.* Under
a cloudy sky, two
young witches are
posed in a manner
usually reserved for
portrayals of the
Three Graces; but
the third figure here
is an infant with a
knowing look and a
storm-spouting
device; and a goat
with a staring eye,
debauched or mad,
serves the plumper
maiden for a seat.

wicked woman he concludes: *All wickedness is but little to the wickedness of a woman.* Wherefore S. John Chrysostom says on the text, 'It is not good to marry' (S. Matthew xix) [the ninety homilies on S Matthew, written about the year 390]: *What else is woman but a foe to friendship, an unescapable punishment, a necessary evil, a natural temptation, a desirable calamity, a domestic danger, a delectable detriment, an evil of nature, painted in fair colours!"*

The real problem, though, was that in addition to being natural temptations and delectable detriments, not to mention evils of nature, women (as the Church never tired of teaching) were also insatiably lustful, and thus could rarely resist the Devil's sexual invitations. Females as young as four years old were proved to have had sexual relations with demons, and were duly punished by the inquisitors. One witch confessed that her own amour with the Devil had begun *in utero*—while she was still a fetus—

Left: *An early woodcut shows a woman in a suggestive rural encounter: with a devil who is jauntily hatted, and decently attired in his upper, but not lower parts. An unpopulated landscape, with a distant church or castle, mere and clipped tree, is the impassive witness to their scandal.*

Below: *A pretty and well-to-do woman makes mouths in a glass, but would see there, if her vanity permitted, only the Devil. Thus woman's frailty, the didact says.*

almost exclusively into contact with women. These he was obliged, by Christian charity and a regard for the state's security, to torture, strip naked, shave from head to toe, and probe for incriminating signs of witchcraft. If any wondered why all the witches were women, and all the inquisitors men, there were explanations, and they were supplied in the witchfinders' primary manual, the *Malleus Maleficarum (The Hammer of Witches)*, written by the German inquisitors Jakob Sprenger and Heinrich Kramer in 1487. Under the heading, "Concerning Witches who Copulate with Devils," Sprenger and Kramer addressed the question *Why is it that Women are chiefly addicted to Evil Superstitions?* and found these answers:

"Now the wickedness of women is spoken of in Ecclesiasticus xxv: *I had rather keep house with a lion and a dragon than to keep house with a wicked woman.* And among much which in that place precedes and follows about a

Above:
The Conjurer *by*
Hieronymous Bosch.
From a basket at
the conjurer's waist
peeps the witch's
symbol, a small
owl.

Opposite above:
Horned beast in
fruiting plenty:
mosaic, 5th century
AD.

Opposite below:
The alchemical spirit
Mercurius, from a
15th-century text.

and her shocked inquisitors soberly
noted the detail for their armory.

A Universal Behavior
A broader definition views witchcraft as
an ancient and universal behavior, whose
history is often inseparable from the
moral and political opposition it has
inspired. In this view, a witch is one who
seeks supernatural powers, of much the
same kind as those described above, and
uses them for good or evil purposes. In
the broad view, a witch's methods are
usually ecstatic rather than ascetic,
instinctive rather than the rational, following the tradition of Dionysus and his
entourage from Ancient Greece. Often,
a powerful witch was employed by the
state, usually for his or her divinatory
powers, and was only persecuted if he or
she fell foul of the authorities or became
a threat to them.

Seers, magicians, shamans, demon-
worshippers, witchdoctors, alchemists,
mediums and all manner of other seekers after occult power fall within the
broad province of witchcraft, though not
all of those described—or prosecuted—
as witches sought occult power. As well
as spell-casters and midnight coveners,
as well as the magical healers, demonists
and devil-possessed nuns, the mediums,
necromancers, and lycanthropes, the
Australian bone-pointers, the flesh-eat-
ing *dakinis* of the Himalayas, the
Babylonian haruspicators, seeking omens
in entrails of sacrificed animals, as well
as the ecstatic voodoo priestesses of the
Caribbean, many persons with far
weaker occult connections, or none at
all, have been dragged screaming into
the witchy fold.

Heretics, for example, like the Albigensians and Waldenses, are found there,

along with worshippers of unfashionable gods; so are mild prophets, of the tea-leaf-reading and crystal-gazing kind, victims of neighborly malice, and unsociable eccentrics. A good many of the raving mad and the drug-deluded have felt the inquisitor's prod, and so have herbalists, midwives and others rash enough to claim, or demonstrate, unorthodox knowledge. Some of those too ostentatiously lacking political correctness have found their place in the witches' roster, and another group, perhaps the smallest in the whole taxonomy of witchcraft, consists of those who have shown some unbidden strain of psychism. Agnes Sampson, who demonstrated this to King James I during the North Berwick witch trials, and so helped herself to the stake (see chapter 4), may have been one of these, and so perhaps was Robert Nixon, another commoner who came too close to an English King.

The Cheshire Plowboy, as Nixon was known, was born around 1467. He was generally thought to be rather stupid, and he sometimes babbled or ranted incomprehensibly to himself. One day, he stopped his plowing, looked around

Mercuriusphorum

THE HARVEST GOAT

Until recently it was common in some parts of Europe for farmers to warn their children not to go into the fields when harvest-time approached. They didn't do it to protect their crops, but because the Corn Goat (or the Oats, or Rye Goat) might snatch the children away, or even kill them, as they played among the golden stalks.

From Norway and Scotland to Estonia, Germany, France, Switzerland and Austria, ripe crops were thought to be guarded by a goat spirit, or goat-like being. The last sheaf to be cut on a farm was often called "the goat," and was sometimes given the rough shape of a goat. In parts of Switzerland, whoever cut the last sheaf, or drove the last harvest wagon load into the barn, was called "the goat," and like a real goat, had a bell tied round his or her neck before being drenched with alcohol. In some areas, the spirit of the harvest goat was thought to lurk among the sheaves in the barn; when the last sheaf was reached at threshing time, it was sometimes decorated with flowers and cakes, and then had the harvest-spirit violently flailed out of it. Around Grenoble, in France, it was the custom towards harvest's end to decorate a goat with flowers and ribbons and set it loose in the field. Then the reapers chased and caught it, killed it, and served its meat as a harvest supper, after first setting aside a piece of the flesh to be pickled and kept till the next year's harvest.

In such forms the ancient goat-gods survived in European fields, guarantors of the crops' fertility, an atavism unsanctioned and unsanctified by the Church.

Above: The burning of Waldensian heretics. The Church's first determined campaign against those with their own ideas occurred in France in the early 13th century, when Waldensians, followers of the dualistic Manichean doctrine, were put to the stake. Here two victims burn and pray, officially observed, and well-guarded by armed men lest they leap from the flames.

Opposite:
The witch as a cartoon; from Punch *magazine, 1911.*

in a startled way, and said a few words that for once made sense. He said: "Now Dick! Now Harry! Oh, ill done, Dick! Oh, well done Harry! Harry has gained the day!" Before long, his meaning became clear: at the moment of his outburst, King Richard III ("Dick") had been defeated by Henry Bolingbroke ("Harry") at the battle of Bosworth Field. News of the plowboy's vision reached King Henry, and he sent an envoy to bring Robert to London.

Robert seemed to know the envoy was coming. He was terrified, and said he was going to be starved to death. To no avail. He was hauled off to London, and examined personally by the king. He had lost a diamond, Henry said, and could Robert help him find it? Robert coolly replied "Those who hide can find." Since Henry had indeed hidden the diamond himself, he was much impressed, and directed that everything Robert said be recorded. Duly interpreted, Robert seemed to forecast wars, deaths and abdications. He also still claimed that he was going to be starved to death, so Henry ordered that

he be given all the food he wanted, whenever he wanted it. This was annoying to the kitchen staff, evidently a surly crew, so whenever Henry left London he charged one of his officers with Robert's safety. One day this officer was suddenly called away himself, so he locked Robert in the King's own rooms for safekeeping. Unfortunately, he forgot to tell anyone what he had done, and, when Robert was finally discovered, it was found that, as he had predicted, he had starved to death.

In the chapters that follow we shall meet witches from all over the world, Robert Nixons and Medeas alike, witchfinders, demonologists, and their political masters, and those few who have heroically opposed the urge to burn. We shall explore witchcraft according to theological, anthropological, psychological, pharmacological, paranormal, feminist, and other schools of thought. And as the second millennium approaches, we shall also consider the neo-Satanists, in their own testimony and according to those whose numbers increase, and who are ever more alert, the neo-witchfinders.

Ancient Demons, Archaic Gods

I form the light and create darkness: I make peace and create evil:
I the Lord do all these things.

—Isaiah 45:7 (A.V.)

One of the earliest accounts of creation, the Babylonian-Assyrian *Enuma Elish*, dating from about 2000 BC, tells how Apsu, the First Begetter, and the Tiamat, the First Mother, produced a generation of dragons from Chaos. In time, a second generation arose, one of whom, a god of wisdom named Ea, killed Apsu. Tiamat and one of her sons, Kingu, produced a race of scorpion-tailed monsters, and Tiamat set out to avenge herself on Ea. She had a company of eleven monsters, and met Ea's son Marduk in battle. But Marduk was armed with seven winds, a storm chariot and a fearsome coat of mail. He wore a red paste on his lips, and on his wrist an herb that protected him from poison. Flames crowned his head.

When they met, Marduk caught Tiamat in a net. He sent a wind into her belly that ripped her open. Then he shot her with arrows and beat her about the head till she was dead. He bound her body and stood on it. Then he shackled the eleven monsters and threw them into an underground prison. They became the gods of the underworld.

Then Marduk split fallen Tiamat's corpse in two, like a shell-fish. He used one half to hold back the waters that were above, and the other as a foundation for the earth and sea. He made the sun, moon, constellations and planets. He went on to kill Kingu, and then to make the human race from his blood.

One of the first of these humans to encounter the underworld gods was

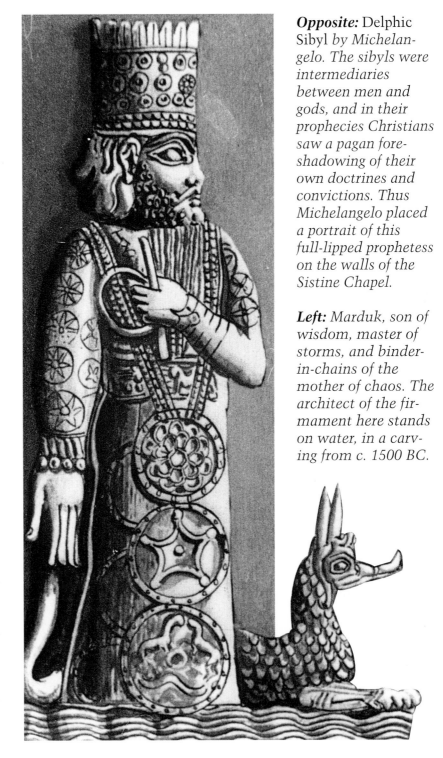

Opposite: Delphic Sibyl *by Michelangelo. The sibyls were intermediaries between men and gods, and in their prophecies Christians saw a pagan foreshadowing of their own doctrines and convictions. Thus Michelangelo placed a portrait of this full-lipped prophetess on the walls of the Sistine Chapel.*

Left: Marduk, son of wisdom, master of storms, and binder-in-chains of the mother of chaos. The architect of the firmament here stands on water, in a carving from c. 1500 BC.

Right: Gilgamesh, the first hero to seek knowledge of an after-life, is shown with his bow and with one of the lions he slew (after praying for the moon god's help), while searching for the herb of immortality; drawing of an alabaster relief.

Opposite: A Goat God with fine horns, furry legs, and flowering head-piece; he is winged, and bears a representation of entwined snakes on his abdomen—two tokens of his spiritual power

Gilgamesh, the hero of a Sumerian-Babylonian epic dating from the third millennium BC. Seeking the herb which could bring him immortality, he finds his way blocked by two fearful beings, one male and one female. They are part human and part dragon, and have tails like scorpions. They recognize that Gilgamesh is partly divine, and let him pass. He eventually enters a paradisal garden and meets a woman there who makes wine. He speaks with Utnapishtim, the Sumerian Noah, who has himself attained immortality, and at last finds the plant he seeks beneath the sea. But a serpent steals it away from him, and he resigns himself to death.

Wily Serpents and Willful Females

The themes first stated in these Mesopotamian epics—dragon-tailed monsters, reeking of the underworld but guarding paradisal gardens where magical plants grow, women who bring mischief into the world—recur with remarkable consistency through four thousand years of occult speculation. Aztec mythology, for instance, echoing Sumerian themes, describes a wonderful garden guarded by a serpent; in the Norse pantheon, a giant snake lies coiled round the base of the world tree, *Ygdrasil*; the serpent's role in Eden is well known, and so is the weakness of Eve, whose disobedience brought woe into the world.

Less well known is the rabbinical tradition in which Eve was created, not from Adam's rib, but from the barbed tail which he originally had, thus converting the demonic element in Adam into female form. That the first target of misogyny was so formed would not have surprised the European witch-hunters, or those late medieval artists who portrayed the serpent in Eden with a woman's face.

Although Eve was the author of Man's downfall, she still was an improvement on Lilith, Adam's first wife in rabbinical tradition. A primordial loose woman, and probably a hussy too, she objected to her supine role in intercourse. "Why must I lie beneath you?" she asked Adam, and when he tried to force her, she quit him and went to live by the Red Sea with more congenially lustful devils. But before she left Adam she bore Asmodeus and other demons. Some say she went on to be a queen in Zmargad and Sheba (Solomon, the wisest of men, thought the Queen of Sheba might be a night-demon because she had hairy legs). She is the same person as the Babylonian-Assyrian wind-demoness Lilitu, known to the Sumerians as Lillake, and a Sumerian text has her living in a willow tree for a while. She strangles infants (contemporary cautions frequently link abortion and witchcraft— see chapter 8), and she is an old hand at the succubus game: no man who sleeps

GOAT GODS AND DANGEROUS WOMEN

The fantasies of the witches' Sabbat, which so intrigued and titillated the renaissance witch-hunters, and of which their victims, under the tutelage of torture, produced remarkably consistent accounts, has its closest counterpart in the Dionysian revels of ancient Greece.

There were three principal classes of persons in the Dionysian entourage. These were the male *sileni* and *satyrs*, and the female *maenads*. The sileni were partly human and partly horse; they walked on two legs, but had hoofs instead of feet; they often had horses' ears, and always horses' tails. The satyrs were goat-men, who lived in wild places. Inveterate molesters of nymphs, naiads and other females, they were clansmen of the musical goat-god Pan, the son of Hermes (the god who turned Dionysus into a young goat to save him from Hera's wrath). Unruly by nature, the satyrs embodied a kind of rural anarchy longed for by those romantics, usually male, who felt diminished by the constraints of an effete civilization. The German philosopher Nietzsche spoke for such would-be wild men in his 1872 essay *The Birth of Tragedy from the Spirit of Music*:

"The satyr, like the idyllic shepherd of our more recent time, is the offspring of a longing for the Primitive and the Natural…Nature, as yet unchanged by knowledge, maintaining impregnable barriers to culture—that was how the Greek saw his satyr, which nevertheless was not to be confused with the primitive cave-man. On the contrary, the satyr was the archetype of man, embodiment of the highest and intensest emotions, the ecstatic reveler enraptured by the proximity of his god…wisdom's harbinger speaking from the heart of nature, emblem of the sexual omnipotence of nature, which the Greek was wont to contemplate with reverence and wonder."

The third class of Dionysiacs were the athletic, snake-eating and promiscuous maenads, literally "ravers." They wore fawn skins or furs, and were drinkers of spruce beer spiked with ivy and honey. Each carried a ritual staff called a *thyrsus*, which was twined around with vine and ivy leaves, and phallically topped with a pine cone. With this interesting device a maenad need only strike the ground to make a spring of wine or water flow; she could also make milk spurt from her fingertips, and the leaves of her staff yielded drops of honey. On the down side, the maenads were excitable. As the Roman historian Plutarch—himself a devotee of Dionysus/Bacchus—explained in his *Roman Questions*:

"…women possessed by Bacchic frenzies rush straightway for the ivy and tear it to pieces, clutching it in their hands and biting it with their teeth….Ivy, possessing as it does an exciting and distracting breath of madness, deranges and agitates them and in general brings on a wineless drunkenness and joyousness in those that are precariously disposed towards spiritual exaltation."

Even worse than their "precarious" spiritual tendencies, the maenads could be downright murderous. Their specialty was to tear living animals and men apart with their bare hands, and this was the fate of Apollo's priest Orpheus. The maenads tossed his severed head into the river Hebrus, but the head, indefatigably musical, continued singing while it was borne out to sea, and eventually came to rest on the island of Lesbos.

The maenads would thus have actually fulfilled the very worst nightmares projected by the Christian witch-hunters on their victims. They were independent and were no respecters of men (least of all of priests and kings), consorting with hairy, cloven-hoofed familiars, and easily induced to frenzy by a horned god. What else could they be, if only in the dreams and nightmares of the witch-hunters, but the spiritual forebears of Europe's supposed witches?

LILITH IN THE WILLOW TREE

Once upon a time the Sumerian goddess Innana was walking by the river Euphrates. She took a fancy to a *huluppu-*tree (perhaps a willow) that was growing there, and carried it back to her garden in the city of Erech. When it grew big, she planned to make a couch and a chair from its wood.

She took good care of the tree, but when the time came to cut it down, she found a great snake called "Knows No Charm" curled up at its base, and nesting in the top branches the bird called *Imdugud*, which decrees fates. And in the middle of it, she found that Lilith, possibly in need of solitude after years of consorting with demons by the dusty shores of the Red Sea, had made her house.

The hero Gilgamesh heard of Inanna's predicament. He strapped on his armor, took up his great axe, and killed the serpent. *Imdugud* flew away to the mountains, and Lilith destroyed her house and took herself off to live in desolate places.

Gilgamesh and the men of Erech cut down the *huluppu-*tree, and Inanna made a drum and a drumstick from its wood.

Inanna is also called Ishtar and Astaroth. She is the Queen of Heaven, the goddess of love, lust and war, and is the consort of the shepherd god Dumuzi, or Tammuz, who is associated with Dionysus. Thus Lilith, the wild first woman, lived for a while in a tree connected, by proxy, with Dionysus, and then in the desert of Edom with his satyrs.

alone is ever quite safe from her.

According to Isaiah (34:11-15), Lilith, whom the King James Version of the Bible refers to simply as a "screech owl"—in Latin *strix*, believed to suck the blood of children, and cognate with *striga*, the word for a witch —and who is simply a "night monster" in the Hebrew Bible, lives in the ruined desert of Edom. She keeps company with pelicans, hedgehogs, owls, ravens, jackals, ostriches, kites, wildcats, hyenas, vipers, and with satyrs, who call to each other in a sad fashion. She also appears in the book of Job (18:13-15), where her circumstances are more domestic and her company is a major underworld figure:

"He [the wicked man] is torn from the shelter of his tent, and dragged before the King of Terrors.
Then Lilith makes her home under his roof, while people scatter brimstone on his holding."

In the Jewish Bible, Lilith appears in this verse as an alien—"that which is none of his."

The scene changes, and we see Job receiving a messenger. The Sabbaeans, he is told, have stolen all his cattle and killed his servants. The story is scarcely finished when another messenger arrives: the "fire of God" has burned up all Job's sheep and killed his shepherds. Then more bad news: the Chaldeans have stolen Job's camels and killed his servants. Then another messenger: Job's sons and daughters were at their eldest brother's house, eating a meal and drinking wine, "when suddenly from the wilderness a gale sprang up, and it battered all four corners of the house, which fell in on the young people. They are dead: I alone escaped to tell you."

But Job blesses the name of Yahweh. Satan again comes to Yahweh. He

Left: Adam's first wife, Lilith (here in her Sumerian form as Lilitu), was made by God from inferior stuff, and went to the bad.

Opposite: Adam and Eve, tempted and expelled from Eden; by Michelangelo, Sistine Chapel

Below: Offering to Job by Laurent de la Hire: the patriarch in his heyday.

Hostile Angels

Although Lucifer appears early in the Bible as a proud and fallen angel, Satan initially serves God as the angel who tests or "accuses" mankind: in Hebrew the word "Satan" means "accuser", only later did it become a personal name. In the first chapter of the Book of Job, Satan is among the Sons of God who "came to attend on Yahweh." Yahweh asks him where he has been, and Satan says he has been "roaming about" the earth. Then he must have seen that God-fearing man Job, God says, and Satan replies that he has—but that Job is only God-fearing because God has blessed him:

"'But stretch out your hand and lay a finger on his possessions: I warrant you, he will curse you to your face.' 'Very well,' Yahweh said to Satan, 'all he has is in your power. But keep your hands off his person.' So Satan left the presence of Yahweh." [Job 3: 1 ff]

Right: *Job, covered with boils from top to toe—down on his luck, but reclining patiently; from a 12th-century miniature.*

Below: The Temptation of Christ *by Duccio: the upstart Satan is rebuked for putting his God to the test.*

admits that Job has passed the test; but just let his health suffer, he threatens, Yahweh will hear himself cursed: "Very well," Yahweh said to Satan, "he is in your power. But spare his life."

Now Job's tribulations begin in earnest. But he survives the Satanic test well enough to retain Yahweh's favor, and eventually obtains more property and children, and lives to a ripe age. As the theology of witchcraft was careful to stress, evil always occurs with God's permission. Satan, as God's *agent provocateur*, always acts within His brief.

Even Christ's own encounters with the devil have a curiously legal quality. In rejecting the penultimate temptation (to throw himself from a parapet of the Temple), he quotes precedent: "It has been said *You must not put the Lord your God to the test.*" His response to the last temptation, the offer of all worldly power, is also by the book. "Be off, Satan!" he replies, "for scripture says *You must worship the Lord your God and serve him alone.*" (Matthew 4:1-11, Luke 4:1-13)

The identity of Satan with the serpent in Eden and with Lucifer seems not to have been established until the end of the first century AD, when the Book of

Revelations was written:

"The great dragon, the primeval serpent, known as the devil or Satan, who had deceived all the world, was hurled down to the earth and his angels were hurled down with him." [Revelations 12:9]

Henceforth, the scaly-tailed, claw-footed, bat- or dragon-winged iconography of Satan becomes, like the Pauline doctrine of original sin, a fixed point in Christian theology. It also develops as a principal preoccupation of the witch-hunters.

In Genesis no such connection is made between the serpent and Satan. The serpent is simply introduced (Genesis 3:1) as "the most subtle of all the wild beasts that Yahweh God had made." A rabbinical tradition, recorded in *The Life of Adam and Eve*, a Jewish text dating from the first century BC, does, however, associate the serpent with Samael, the angel who rebels when Yahweh orders the heavenly host to worship Adam, his new creation. When Michael warns him that his disobedience will provoke God's anger, Samael (the name is said to mean 'Venom of God' or to be

a corruption of Shemel, the name of a Syrian deity) says that in that case he will build a throne above the stars and proclaim himself the highest of all beings. His angels rally round in agreement, and the Archangel promptly throws them all out of heaven and down into a deep dark dungeon. In the apocryphal *Second Book of Enoch*, dating from the first century BC, these fallen angels are known as the Watchers.

WHERE VISIONS COME FROM: THE ORGAN OF PROPHECY

The liver was thought by the Greeks and other ancient peoples to be the organ of prophecy. Plato gives the following account in his *Timaeus* of how this came about:

The appetite for food and drink and other natural needs of the body they located between the midriff and the region of the navel, building in the area a kind of manger for the body's food; and they secured appetite there like a wild beast....in order that it might feed at its stall, but be as far as possible from the seat of deliberation, and cause the least possible noise and disturbance, so leaving the highest part of us to deliberate quietly about the welfare of each and all.

And knowing that it would not understand reason or be capable of paying attention to rational argument even if it became aware of it, but would easily fall under the sway of images and phantoms by day or night, god played upon this weakness and formed the liver, which he put into the creature's stall. He made it smooth and close in texture, sweet and bitter, so that the influence of the mind could project thoughts upon it which it would receive and reflect in the form of visible images, like a mirror.

When the mind wants to cause fear, it makes use of the liver's native bitterness and plays a stern and threatening role, quickly infusing the whole organ with bitterness and giving it a bilious colour; at the same time it contracts the liver and makes it all wrinkled and rough, bending and shrivelling the lobe, blocking and closing the vessels leading to it and so causing pain and nausea.

By contrast gentle thoughts from the mind produce images of the opposite kind...using the organ's innate sweetness to render it straight and smooth and free, and making the part of the soul that lives in the region of the liver cheerful and gentle, and able to spend the night quietly in divination and dreams, as reason and understanding are beyond it.

Such then is the nature and position of the liver, which enables it to carry out its function of prophecy.

Above, left: The Archangel Michael and well-armed adjutants put down demons with goat heads and reptilian bodies.

Right: Egyptian bronze cat, c. 663-525 BC. Cats were the associates of Egyptian and Norse gods, and of English and Scottish witches—as common domestic animals, they were usually at hand when a witchfinder needed to identify his suspect's familiar.

Below: Moses, with Yahweh's help, turns his staff into a snake; Pharaoh, with effete magicians, is dismayed. From a Victorian lantern slide.

Sorcery Proscribed and Endorsed

Yahweh proscribed sorcery and divination on pain of death: Exodus 22:18 "You shall not allow a sorceress to live"—though in the Greek Septuagint the word translated here as "sorceress" is "pharmakos," primarily meaning "poisoner"; Leviticus 20:27: "Any man or woman who is a necromancer or magician must be put to death by stoning; their blood shall be on their own heads." And Deuteronomy 18:10-11: "There must never be anyone among you…who practises divination, who is a soothsayer, augur or sorcerer, who uses charms, consults ghosts or spirits, or calls up the dead."

But the Exodus from Egypt could not have been accomplished without numerous feats of sanctioned magic. The most famous of these, involving a contest with Egyptian magicians, is described in Exodus 7:9-13:

"Yahweh said to Moses and Aaron, "If Pharaoh says to you, 'Produce some marvel,' you must say to Aaron, 'Take your staff and throw it down in front of Pharaoh, and let it turn into a serpent.'

To Pharaoh then Moses and Aaron duly went, and they did as Yahweh commanded. Aaron threw down his staff in front of Pharaoh, and it turned into a serpent.

Then Pharaoh in his turn called for the sages and the sorcerers, and with their witchcraft the magicians of Egypt did the same,

Each threw his staff down and these turned into serpents. But Aaron's staff swallowed up the staffs of the magicians.

Yet Pharaoh's heart was stubborn and, as Yahweh had foretold, he would not listen to Moses and Aaron."

Moses and Aaron then follow Yahweh's further instructions and use their staffs to inflict plagues on Egypt. Pharaoh's magicians match them in turning rivers into blood and creating a plague of frogs, but are outclassed when it comes to the plagues of mosquitoes and gadflies, the

Left: Moses *by Michelangelo, horned like Bacchus. Renaissance Neoplatonists linked the great prophet of Yahweh to the drunken vine god on the basis of Biblical texts (and their cabalistic interpretation), describing the intoxicating quality of God's presence and the uniquely direct nature of the relationship between God and Moses (Numbers 12:7 ff.). This identification was later taken by anti-Semites to prove a demonic element in Moses' character, just as the horned Bacchus-Dionysus family became a prototype of the Christian Devil. But Michelangelo, not ignorant of Renaissance philosophy, intended to convey by the horns of Moses a token of spiritual attainment matching the prophet's physical grandeur.*

death of livestock, the visitations of boils, hail, locusts, and darkness, and the death of Egypt's first-born.

Moses later uses his magical staff to make water flow from the desert rock, and when the Israelites do battle with the Amalekites they prevail as long as Moses holds his staff aloft. But when they later face the Midianite and Amalekite armies, Yahweh is anxious lest their victory be misinterpreted:

"Then Yahweh said to Gideon, "there are too many people with you for me to put the Midian into their power; Israel might claim the credit for themselves at my expense: they might say, 'My own hand has rescued me.'" [Judges 7:2]

So Yahweh tells Gideon to let all those who are afraid of the coming battle go home, and 22,000 Israelites leave the field. But the 10,000 remaining are still too many, so Yahweh has Gideon lead them down to the river to drink. Some lap the water like dogs, and some kneel to drink. Of the former there are 300, and Yahweh orders Gideon to choose only these for the coming battle.

Now the odds are truly formidable. The Midianites and their allies "stretched through the valley as thick as locusts; their camels were innumerable like the sand on the seashore." But Yahweh procures a victory for the Israelites, by the simple expedient of causing the enemy troops to slaughter each other.

In critical circumstances it was especially important that free-lance diviners and magicians not be allowed to obscure official policy. Thus, when King Saul was pressed by the Philistines, he enforced the ban on necromancy, and expelled the sorcerers. Then he applied to Yahweh for advice [1 Samuel 28:6], but when the Lord "gave him no answer, either by dream or oracle or prophet," he was obliged to find himself a witch. At his request she raises the ghost of

Samuel, who correctly forecasts Saul's imminent death.

As well as necromancy and wand-power, other occult procedures were well known in the ancient middle east, including the interpretation of dreams, the casting of lots (*urim* and *thummin*), and methods of sympathetic magic involving magical models, the "poppets" that are a traditional part of the witch's armory. When the Philistines captured the Ark of God near Ebenezer, they set it next to the statue of Dagon in their temple. The next morning they found the statue prostrate before the Ark.

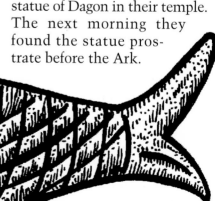

The priests replaced it, but by morning Dagon was on the floor again, this time with his head and hands broken off. Next, a plague of tumors and rats struck the Philistines, and soon they wanted nothing more than to get rid of the Ark.

Their priests and diviners told them how to do it: the Ark must be sent back to the Israelites, along with golden models of the rats and tumors. This was done, and the rats and tumors departed with the golden models.

Classical Sorcery
One of the most successful and influential magicians of the ancient world was the pharaoh Nekhtanebf II, who is said to have protected his kingdom by witchcraft from 359 to 342 BC. His method was as follows. News of an attack comes: an invading fleet is standing off the Nile delta. The King seems unperturbed, but soon he goes to the secret room where he does magic. He pours pure water into a great bowl, and on its surface floats small wax models of the ships in his own and the enemy fleet. He says the words of power, summoning demons of the wind and other elements. The toy fleets begin to move. They engage each other, waves roughen the surface of the water, and soon the models of the invaders' ships begin to founder. As they do, their counterparts founder and sink in the Mediterranean. Egypt has been saved again.

But then a day comes when a Persian force gathers against Egypt. Nekhtanebf goes to the secret room. He tries the words of power, but now his magic is insufficient. He foresees his troops defeated, sees Egypt over-run by Artaxerxes Ochus, the butcher. No choice remains, so the Pharaoh puts on a disguise, and taking with him only gold and his books of magic, he flees. At length he crosses the Mediterranean and settles in Macedonia, where his reputation as a doctor and seer spreads. He has brought the Egyptian arts of magic and divination to Greece.

Above: *Hybrid demons, the clawed and hoofed offspring of earth and sky, with probing tongues and heavy fangs, endure, and provoke, stormy conditions*

29

THE WITCH OF ENDOR

Necromancy—consultation with the spirits of the dead—was not forbidden by Yahweh as a mere superstition. It was sometimes, as for Saul in his time of crisis, an effective last resort:

"Then Saul said to his servants, 'Find a woman who is a necromancer for me to go and consult her.' His servants replied, 'There is a necromancer at En-dor.'

And so Saul, disguising himself and changing his clothes, set out accompanied by two men; their visit to the woman took place at night. 'Disclose the future to me' he said 'by means of a ghost.' The woman answered, 'Look, you know what Saul has done, how he has swept the necromancers and wizards out of the country; why are you setting a trap for my life, then, to have me killed?' But Saul swore to her by Yahweh, 'As Yahweh lives,' he said 'no blame shall attach to you for this business.'
Then the woman asked, 'Whom shall I conjure up for you?' He replied, 'Conjure up Samuel.'

The woman saw Samuel and, giving a great cry, she said to Saul, 'Why have you deceived me? You are Saul.' The King said, 'Do not be afraid! What do you see?' The woman answered Saul, 'I see a ghost rising up from the earth.' 'What is he like?' he asked. She answered, 'It is an old man coming up; he is wrapped in a cloak.' Then Saul knew it was Samuel and he bowed down his face to the ground and did homage.

Then Samuel said to Saul, 'Why have you disturbed my rest, conjuring me up?' Saul replied, 'I am in great distress; the Philistines are waging war against me, and God has abandoned me and no longer answers me by prophet or dream; and so I have summoned you to tell me what I must do.' Samuel said, 'And why do you consult me, when Yahweh has abandoned you and is with your neighbor? Yahweh has done to you as he foretold through me; he has snatched the sovereignty from your hand and given it to your neighbor, David, because you disobeyed the voice of Yahweh and did not execute his fierce anger against Amalek. That is why Yahweh treats you like this now. What is more, Yahweh will deliver Israel and you, too, into the power of the Philistines.'" [[1 Samuel 28:8-19]

Samuel is correct, of course, and the next day Saul is wounded by bowmen and takes his own life.

The Strategies of Witchcraft

The story of Nekhtanebf's witchcraft includes three elements that recur throughout the subject's history: a theme of political crisis, the agency of supernatural powers, and the exploitation of a mysterious link between things similar but different—here, the wax models and the ships they represent.

The principal political element of ancient witchcraft was divination, and state oracles were well established throughout the classical world. Among the Mesopotamians, haruspication, the study of the internal organs of sacrificed animals, seems to have been the most common method of augury, but abnormal or monstrous births, both human and animal, were also scrutinized by *baruas* or entrail specialists. Dreams, which the Sumerians recognized as the province of the dream-god or night demon *An-Za-Qar*, were also widely studied for their predictive power. Thus the earliest means of divination involved both ritual sacrifice (or murder—in Rome, the use of humans for haruspication had to be specifically outlawed), or the invocation of a supernatural being.

In China, and elsewhere, essentially similar techniques interpreted such seemingly random phenomena as the lines on tortoise shells, flights of birds, the cracks appearing in burned bones or the way a handful of sticks and stones fell. Tea-leaves and playing cards are still used in the same way. In all such divinations a connection, either cosmological or established by some superior agency, is assumed between the immediate small-scale event and whatever it predicts.

The major oracles of ancient Greece were institutions with enduring social and political weight. The Oracle of Apollo at Delphi, on the slopes of Mount Parnassus, is the most famous of these today, but others were equally renowned. The temple of Ammon, in what is now Libya, but which originally lay in the territory known as Nubia, was one of the most eminent, and the oak grove sacred to Zeus at Dodona was another. Every

Opposite: Saul and the Witch of Endor *by Benjamin West.*

Below: Roman Augurs, *perhaps amused by the tricks of fate that lend their utterance official weight, share a private moment in the company of their oracular caged birds.*

Below, left: Mural *from the Tomb of the Auguri, Tarquinia. A warrior dances across the wall, accompanied by birds; according to their flight, official strategies were planned.*

oracle had its staff of priests, and though open, for a fee, to the public, each was in some way subsidized by the state. Methods of divination varied. At Dodona many different kinds were used, one of the most popular being kleromancy—the provision of a yes-no answer to questions suitably phrased and written on strips of lead. At Ammon, answers were disclosed by movements of the god's statue, duly interpreted by his priests.

At Delphi, where Apollo, the god of light, had vanquished a great serpent, oracular statements were delivered by a priestess known as the Pythia. In some accounts she sat on a tripod above a crack in the earth, inhaling volcanic fumes (or perhaps the fumes of decay rising from the body of the dead serpent) and the smoke from a burning mixture of barley, marijuana and chopped bay leaves. She spoke in verse, and her words had to be interpreted by trained priests. (Though some say these details are a late addition, and that Pythia spoke clearly, though not unambiguously, to those who paid her fee.) During the fourth and fifth centuries BC, a consultation cost private citizens an amount equal to two days' pay

for an average Athenian, and states were charged ten times as much. Emergency consultations were available (three Pythias worked in shifts at the oracle), but at a premium price.

Non-institutional advice on hidden things was also available, but at a greater psychic risk, from witches, and by necromantic procedures that could be really dangerous. When the hero Odysseus needs prophetic advice from the great, but dead, seer Teiresias, he seeks counsel from Circe, the enchantress who has

already turned several of his crew into pigs. She tells him that to find Teiresias he must first visit Persephone's groves of willow and black poplar skirting the House of Hades. He does so, and there digs a pit one cubit square; he pours a libation of honey, milk, wine and water, and sprinkles white barley meal over it; then fills the pit with the blood of a ram and a black ewe sacrificed to Hades and Persephone.

Guerrilla Witchcraft: Wild Gods and Raving Women

If the oracles of Apollo at Delphi and Zeus at Dodona were typical of established Greek religion, a more personal, anarchic, and ecstatic impulse was expressed in the worship of Dionysus, the horned god of wine and fertility. He stood in somewhat the same relation to the more senior gods of Olympus as Hecate, the frightful patron of necromancers, stood in relation to the Pythia, and those who followed him in his wildest guise were very different from the careful haruspicators of official augury. In their religious frenzy, these devotees did not remove, in a surgical manner, the entrails of sacrificed animals, but tore apart living creatures, including humans, with their teeth and hands.

Dionysus was principally a god of the earth, specifically of the vine. His name in Greek means "sprout (or shoot) of god," and his main festivals, like those of the Corn goddess Demeter, were celebrated at harvest's end. He was half human and half divine, having Zeus for a father and a mortal, Semele, for a

Left: Circe, the witches' witch, changes, or perhaps reverts, the male companions of Odysseus into swine. They have come to her island palace, have seen the wild beasts (other transformed men) prowling around it, and have heard her beautiful singing. She has invited them in and fed them drugged honey, cheese, and wine. Then, with a flick of her wand—they're all grunters, and away to the sties. But Odysseus, herbally immune to her magic, obtains the witch's favors and the restitution of his men.

Below, left: To be rid of Scylla, a rival for the love of the sea-god Glaucus, Circe and her handmaidens enchant the wine-dark sea. By this unsisterly act Scylla was changed into a sea-monster and lurked, with the even more dangerous Charybdis, in the Straits of Messina. There she snatched six of Odysseus' sailors, one in each of her mouths, and retired to eat them at leisure. Or so says Homer (who may well have been a woman, according to some authorities).

Below: *The birth of Dionysus from the thigh of Zeus: the sturdy twice-born makes straight for the arms of Hermes, who will be his invaluable protector.*

Opposite Maenad: *Roman copy of a 5th-century BC Greek statue. She holds the indispensable pine-cone-tipped staff known as the* thyrsus, *with which milk could be charmed from the ground, and opponents felled at a blow.*

mother. His birth was miraculous, and occurred as follows.

Zeus loved Semele, and swore to give her anything she wanted. She asked to see him in his full divine radiance, and by his oath he was so obliged. But Semele was burned up by the brightness of her lover's glory. As she died, Zeus snatched her unborn child from her, and sewed it up in his thigh until the time came for the child to be born. (Thus Dionysus is also called "the doubly born.") Then Zeus had the god Hermes carry the child, who was horned and crowned with snakes, to Mt. Nyssa, to be cared for by nymphs and the drunken Silenus.

When he was a young man Dionysus, driven half-mad by Zeus' still-jealous wife Hera, wandered across the earth, teaching men how to cultivate the vine and worship him. He introduced the vine into Egypt and invited Amazon queens to march with him. He was opposed by the king of Damascus, but flayed him alive and built a bridge of vines and ivy over the river Euphrates. A tiger helped

him across the river Tigris, and after defeating Indian armies he introduced vines to the sub-continent. At length his grandmother, the Titaness Rhea, restored his sanity. He continued to wander, accompanied by goat-legged satyrs, sileni, maenads and nymphs.

On one occasion he came to Thebes with this rabble, and invited the women of the city to join him in revels on Mount Cithaeron. The spectacle and prospect were gravely offensive to King Pentheus, who promptly had the maenads jailed and Dionysus arrested. But the maenads could not be bound, and their cell doors would not stay locked. Dionysus told the king, who was a religious conservative, that he was a god, but Pentheus would have none of it and had him jailed. Naturally, no bonds or jail doors could restrain him, and Dionysus came back to give Pentheus a second chance. Meeting only with threats and insults, he left the king to his fate.

The maenads had taken to the hills with many of the Theban women, includ-

ing Pentheus' mother and sisters. Pentheus set out in pursuit of them. Then Dionysus brought a divine madness upon the women, so that they mistook Pentheus for a mountain lion, and tore him limb from limb, with his mother leading the pack.

This strange half-human god also appears as the Great Hunter, the fully divine Dionysus Zagreus, son of Zeus and Demeter's daughter Persephone. Zeus proposed to make him ruler of the universe, but this infuriated the Titans (those older gods who were the parents of Zeus and the Olympians), and when they caught the young god, they dismembered him, boiled, and ate him. A pomegranate tree, linking him with Adonis and Tammuz, grew on the spot where his blood touched the earth. But Athena, the goddess of Wisdom, rescued the boy's heart and gave it to Zeus. Zeus swallowed the heart, and in time a second Dionysus Zagreus was born from his thigh.

Thus reborn, Dionysus waged war on

Right: *Hermes, swift messenger of the gods, in cloak and bathing suit, carries the infant Dionysus—haloed but sought for his hide by jealous Hera, wife of Zeus— to safety. The young god finds haven, dressed as a girl, in the household of Orchomenus, and then, changed by Hermes into a young goat, on the slopes of Mt. Nyssa, where nymphs tend him. Thereafter, he becomes prejudiced, perhaps understand- ably, towards alco- hol, goats, women, and a wandering life. One of the few gods who was kind to his mother, Dionysus arranged for Semele (his human parent) to be released from Hades and given a place with the gods on Mt. Olympus. The flight scene is from a mosaic at the Villa Antioch-on-the- Orontes, c. AD 225- 250.*

ΔΙΟΝ

the Titans, finally destroying them with lightning bolts. From their ashes humans arose, divine in their Dionysian part, evil in their Titanic inheritance.

In another version of this myth, more reminiscent of the story of how Isis re-assembled the dismembered body of the fertility god Osiris, the body of Dionysus was put together and then resuscitated by his grandmother Rhea. She entrusted him to King Orchomenus, and to safe-guard the boy he was disguised as a girl and brought up in the women's quarters. But Hera, who was still jealous, discov-ered the imposture. She drove Orchome-nus and his queen mad, and would have had her revenge on Dionysus if Hermes had not turned him into a young goat and whisked him off to Mt. Nyssa, to be raised there by nymphs and the boozy Silenus.

In a third form, as Dionysus Bassareus, the god appears wearing fox skins, and his maenad followers wear the spotted fur of wolf-like animals. These women

THE DEATH OF CAESAR

There were several bad signs: wild birds had settled in the Forum; fiery men were seen fighting; a tomb with a sinister plaque had been opened. And when the Roman augur Vestricus Spurinna examined the entrails of a sacrificed animal, he saw March 15 as the high point of danger. On the night of March 14 a wind blew Caesar's bedroom door open, waking his wife from a nightmare in which she held him, dead, in her arms. The next day, Caesar was murdered by his political enemies.

Above: The assassina-tion of Julius Caesar

Left: While still a youth, Dionysus was kidnapped by pirates, who fancied to sell him as a slave. Aboard their ship, they bound him with cords for safekeeping: useless. The cords turned into vines, and climbed up the rig-ging; then Dionysus tossed the pirates into the sea, and changed them into dolphins— all save one, who had urged his release. The vine-clad ship and former crew are shown here in the bowl of a Greek cup.

Right: *A young satyr, wearing an animal skin (its paws are knotted over his chest) and playing a musical pipe. The goat god Pan is perhaps the only deity whose death (gods being mortal like the rest of us) was recorded by humans. A sailor named Thamus was passing the island of Paxi on his way to Italy when he heard a great voice drifting across the water, saying, "Thamus, when you get to Palodes, tell people that the great god Pan is dead!" Thamus did as he was told, and the historian Plutarch recorded the story in his book* Why Oracles are Silent. *Members of Pan's family, however, going by many names—satyrs, fauns and sylvans, for instance—are rumored by some to be alive and well in the world's wild places, though perhaps nervous, like all wild things, of their habitat's destruction.*

Opposite
The Mesopotamian demon Pazuzu.

were also sometimes called *Lyssades*, from a word meaning "rage" or "rabies," and perhaps originally referring to lupine rabies. During the great witch-hunts we shall meet with many witches convicted of, among other things, lycanthropy and werewolfism.

In all the mythologies of Dionysus the recurrent themes are of a god with strong human connections, who is prone to violence, and suffers (is dismembered and resurrected, like the crops whose fertility he oversees). The god is usually horned and accompanied by horned familiars, and his principal followers are wild females, worshipping in fields, woods and ravines instead of established temples. And in the Eleusinian mysteries, which were devoted to Dionysus and Demeter, a mystery religion was developed which gave its devotees confidence in an after-life. As late as 80 BC the historian Plutarch wrote comforting words to his wife after their daughter had died:

"About that which you have heard, dear heart, that the soul once departed from the body vanishes and feels nothing, I know that you give no belief to such assertions because of those sacred and faithful promises given in the mysteries of Bacchus [the Roman name for Dionysus] which we who are of that religious brotherhood know. We hold it firmly for an undoubted truth that our soul is incorruptible and immortal. We are to think [of the dead] that they pass into a better place and a happier condition. Let us behave ourselves accordingly, outwardly ordering our lives, while within all shall be purer, wiser, incorruptible."

In his major features, Dionysus was potent enough, and sufficiently popular, to survive until modern times, in rural and pseudonymous fragments, as a type of the horned, anarchic god. And Satan with him.

HYBRID DEMONS

In the ancient world, hybrids were often looked at with horror, as an unnatural mixing of the established species. The monstrous character of demons was therefore shown by giving them body-parts from all over the animal kingdom. The Sumerian demon Pazuzu, for instance, was shown with an eagle's clawed feet, the head of a lion-like animal, and wings more like an insect's than a bird's. Satan himself suffered a more inadvertent hybridization: in some images he is shown (as the figurative descendant of archaic goat-gods should be), with a goat's horns, legs and feet. But in traditions looking back to the serpent in Eden and to even older reptilian demons of the Middle East, he is shown with the clawed feet and scaly wings of a dragon—and with a pair of horns thrown in for good measure.

Dreams and Visions

Who is there that is not led out of himself in dreams and nocturnal visions, and sees much when dreaming which he had never seen waking?

— CANON EPISCOPI

In the Welsh cycle of heroic and magical tales known as the *Mabinogion*, the story is told of Math, the old king and magician, who (except in battle) could only live "as long as his feet were in the folds of a virgin's lap." We also meet Leu Skillful Hand, his guardian, the trickster Gwydyon, and Blodeuwedd, the woman of flowers.

Now it happened that Leu had been cursed by his mother never to find a wife "of the race that is on earth at this time." But his guardian, Gwydyon, took him to see Math, who made a woman for the young man out of the flowers of oak, broom and meadowsweet. Because of the way she was made, and because she was so beautiful, she was baptized Blodeuwedd, "the flower-faced." She and Leu married, but after a time she fell in love with Goronwy the Staunch, Lord of Pembroke, and he fell in love with her. They schemed for a way to be rid of Leu, which was difficult, because he could only be killed under special circumstances—neither indoors, nor out of doors, neither on foot nor on horseback.

"Then how can you be killed?" Blodeuwedd asked him, pretending to be worried. So because Leu loved her he told her: he could only be killed if someone first made him a bath on a river bank and covered it with a thatched roof; then, if someone drove a goat into the bath house, and managed to catch Leu standing with one foot on the goat and the other on the edge of the bath, they could kill him.

And strangely enough, that's what Blodeuwedd and Goronwy managed to do. And then they married.

But Gwydyon, Leu's guardian, searched for Leu high and low, and at last found him. He had been turned into an eagle, but one whose feathers and flesh were rotting off and being eaten daily by a pig that came to the tree where he perched. Gwydyon coaxed the bird onto his knee, and by touching him with his wand transformed him into Leu again. He was very weak, but doctors cared for him, and he soon regained his strength.

Then Leu and Gwydyon raised an army and marched against Goronwy. When Blodeuwedd heard they were coming, she and her women fled—but the women were all so afraid that they walked backwards, to see who was following them, and they all, except Blodeuwedd, fell into a lake and were drowned. When Gwydyon found Blodeuwedd, he said : "I will not kill you, but I will do what is worse; I will let you go in the form of a bird. Because of the shame you have brought on Leu Skillful Hand, you are never to show your face to the light of day, rather you shall fear other birds; they will be hostile to you, and it will be their nature to maul and molest you wherever they find you. You will not lose your name, but will always be called Blodeuwedd." And he changed her into an owl, and even today the name of an owl in Welsh is "blodeuwedd."

East Meets North

The *Mabinogion* seems to have taken shape about AD 1000, but in its world of romance, magic and Celtic lore, there are far older elements. Specifically, the story of Blodeuwedd is both a magical romance and a redaction of elements pre-

Opposite: *In one of her numerous Welsh legends, Blodeuwedd, who was made from flowers by a magician and married to a sun-god, invites Gronw Pebyr, a god of darkness, into her castle. For her generally faithless dabbling, she was turned into an owl, the witch's alter ego, and shunned by all.*

Below: *A northern warrior, bent on chivalry, is interrupted in the woods by the appearance of a Valkyrie. She dazzles him with a pure and military virtue, and, while her troops breast the trees, a merely human female swoons.*

dating the Genesis story. For example:

The magical creation of a woman: as Yahweh made Lilith to be Adam's first wife, so Math made Blodeuwedd for Leu.
Her evil disposition: Lilith proves to be a bad—sexually disobedient—wife; Blodeuwedd also proves to be disloyal.
The subsequent degradation of her human form: Lilith, as Lamia (the name given to her in the Latin Vulgate translation of the Bible) is reduced by her wickedness from great beauty to bestial ugliness. The beautiful Blodeuwedd is turned into an owl.
Her loathsome reputation and banishment: Lilith lives at first, bird-like, in a tree and later (Isaiah 34) in the desolate desert of Edom; Lamia keeps her eyes in

a box and must make special provisions before she can see. Blodeuwedd will never have company or see the light of day.
Her identification with witchcraft: In the Authorized Version of the Bible, Lilith appears as a screech-owl, whose reputation was to drink the blood of infants (also Lamia's principal crime) and from whose name the Latin word for a witch was derived. Blodeuwedd is, specifically, turned into an owl, a bird with a dark history. During the middle ages it became a bird of ill-omen, and the witch's common companion.

Thus this Celtic tale represents a northward migration of ancient Near Eastern and classical elements, and their trans-

formation, within a native context, into something less sinister than their originals. By the same process the horned gods of the classical world re-appeared in northern Europe as harvest sprites and woodland pagans, and the wild hunt of Dionysus Zagreus was re-enacted in Norse, Teutonic and Celtic legends featuring Odin and the un-reformed—un-Christianized—King Arthur.

At the same time, those ancient beliefs and superstitions were also being transmitted, within a Christian context and in a far more direct fashion, by such fathers of the Church as St. Augustine, whose word had almost canonical force. Once they had been painstakingly woven into the fabric of Catholic theodicy, it required only the social and economic changes of the later middle ages and Renaissance, along with the Reformation and a sharp downturn in the church's political fortunes, to produce a climate for supposed witches that was far harsher than the one in which Math and Gwydyon had performed their magic.

Dreams and Nocturnal Visions

Before those changes took place, the Church's attitude to witchcraft was relatively tolerant, and was defined by the 4th-century article of Church law known as the *Canon episcopi*. Although this begins by urging bishops and their officials to "labor with all their strength to uproot thoroughly from their parishes the pernicious art of sorcery and malefice invented by the devil," it recommends nothing more damaging than that offenders be ejected "foully disgraced from their parishes." The *Canon* also discusses the Sabbat:

"It is also not to be omitted that some wicked women perverted by the devil, seduced by illusions and phantasms of demons, believe and profess, in the hours of night, to ride upon certain beasts with Diana, the goddess of pagans, and innumerable multitudes of women, and in the silence of the dead of night to traverse great spaces of the earth, and to

obey her commands as of their mistress, and to be summoned to her service on certain nights."

But, although such convictions are harmful, the *Canon* says, they are no more than a fantasy:

"Who is there that is not led out of himself in dreams and nocturnal visions, and sees much when sleeping which he had never seen waking? Who is so stupid and foolish as to think that all these things which are done only in spirit happen in the body? It is, therefore, to be proclaimed

Above: The Dream of Reason Gives Birth to Monsters *by Goya: a secular view of the hidden realm, which the Spanish painter personates with an orthodox menagerie of shady bats, staring owls, and a loony cat.*

Below: Witches, haggard but successful, prime their fiery pot with a cockerel and a snake to make a killing hail. Beyond the hill are probably ripe fields of corn, the witches' target.

Opposite: Roots of the male and female mandragora. The plant's roots are rich in tropane alkaloids, and were widely used in the ancient world for aphrodisiac and narcotic purposes; it was grown in the medical gardens of the Babylonian King Mardukapal-Iddina.

publicly that whoever believes such things or similar to these loses the faith, and he who has not the right faith in God is not of God but of him in whom he believes, that is, of the devil."

This sensible doctrine was to give much trouble to witch-hunters during the period of witch-mania, for it not only declared what they prosecuted as a fact to be an illusion, but consigned them, on account of that belief, to be of the devil's party themselves. But this was an inconvenience the Church and judiciaries managed to ignore.

As late as 1020 Burchard, the Bishop of Worms, drew up for his priests a list of suitable punishments for those who practiced or *believed that they could practice* various kinds of sorcery. For example, those who confessed to having believed that they could procure their neighbors' milk and honey for themselves "by their fascinations and incan-

tations," were to be required to do penance on feast days for three years. A woman who believed that: "...a woman in bed in her husband's arms, with the doors closed, can go out and with other women, deceived by similar error, traverse spaces of earth and without arms slay men, baptized and redeemed with Christ's blood, and eat their cooked flesh and replace their hearts with straw and wood or other things and then revive them and give them further life..." was to be punished by "quarantine on bread and water and seven years' penance"— severe enough, but still a far cry from being tortured and burned alive. A person who had "spread a table with meat and drink and three knives" in case "the three sisters" came, was required to do penance on feast days for a year. The three sisters were the Three Fates who spun, measured and cut the thread of life in Greek and Roman mythology; in Norse myth they were known as the Norns, and were goddesses of the Past, Present and Future; they appear as the three witches in Shakespeare's *Macbeth*.

Despite ecclesiastical skepticism (and by no means all churchmen were as doubtful of witchcraft's efficacy as the *Canon episcopi*), belief in various kinds of sorcery remained widespread. Witches were credited with being able, with demonic help, to affect the weather. For instance, by boiling up a pot of noxious herbs and other ingredients, and allowing the fumes to rise into the air, they could "by the power of Satan, and with God's permission" precipitate hail and storms. In 1080 the Pope himself, Gregory VII, was irked enough by such beliefs to write to the King of Denmark complaining that by ascribing bad weather and other misfortunes to the activities of witches (and sinful priests), he merely risked provoking the further wrath of God.

As well as tampering with the weather, witches were also known to make models of wax and other substances (potions of spiders, toads, frogs, snakes and mice), and to perform magic with them. Sacra-

A NOSTRUM FOR WOMEN: TO RID YOURSELVES OF AN AQUEOUS DEMON

A persistent incubus of the aqueous kind once took to troubling a virtuous nun (he assumed the form of a very handsome young man). She was able to free herself from his attentions, however, by having her cell regularly fumigated according to the following prescription (current botanical names have been added):

"[In a new bowl of earthenware and glass put] sweet calamus [*Calamus aromaticus = Acorus aromaticus*, or sweet flag; or, Malabar sweet lemon grass, *Andropogon schoenanthus*], cubeb seed [*Piper cubeba* or *Cubeba officinalis*], roots of both aristolochies [*Aristlochia* species; hartwort and common birthwort], great and small cardamon [*Elettaria cardamomum*; also, loosely, species of *Afromomum & Amomum*], ginger, long pepper [immature fruit spikes of *Piper officinarum & Piper longum*, both said to be used medicinally by Hindus], caryophylleae [clove pinks], cinnamon, cloves, mace nutmegs, calamite storax [*Styrax officinalis*, the medieval source of balsam; the genus is also a source of benzoin], benzoin [probably *Styrax benzoin*], aloeswood and roots, one ounce of fragrant sandal, and three quarts of half brandy and water…set on hot ashes to force forth and upwards the fumigating vapour…"

Although in this way the nun rid her cell of the demon, he then took to following her about whenever she ventured abroad. Upon seeking competent theological advice, however, she was able to deal him a repulsive blow by never failing to carry about her person:

"…pills and pomanders made of the most exquisite perfumes, such as musk, amber, civet, Peruvian balsam, and other essences."

We are in debt for this recipe to the eminent demonologist Ludovco Maria Sinistrari (1622-1701), as recorded in his compendium *De Demonialitate*.

Finally, some words of ancient caution for those preparing their own potions:

Dig up peonies at night: if a woodpecker sees you, it will go for your eyes.

Stand upwind when you pick wild rose hips, or your eyes will swell.

As to mandragora: have a dog pull or dig it up (but not a dog you're fond of—death attends the digging). Be sure to block your ears: the root screams when it comes up, and the sound will drive you mad.

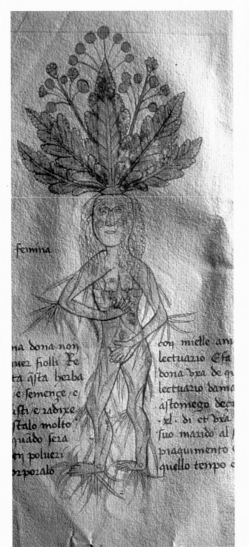

Above: A priest sees all, and could perhaps, like St. Bernard in Nantes, (by extinguishing the church candles) expel the demon that toys with the woman's skirt...but only if she wishes it.

woman, repentant after enjoying the attentions of an incubus for seven years, by giving her his staff to take to bed. The demon was duly repelled, but threatened dire revenge when Bernard and his staff were gone. That Sunday Bernard anathematized the demon from the pulpit, forbidding him access to all human females. As the church candles were extinguished, so were the demon's sexual abilities, until they disappeared entirely. The demon's opinion of this operation is not recorded. It all happened at Nantes, in France, in 1135.

Remedies less suggestive than a saintly staff were also available against incubi. They included prayer (for example *"Sancta Maria, adjuva"*—"Holy Mary, come to my help,") minerals (diamond, jet, jasper, coral), biologicals (the skin of the head of a wolf or ass, menstrual blood, smoke from the burning heart of a fish), and botanicals (rue, St. John's wort, verbena, germander, and Palma Christi, the castor oil plant). In extreme cases, botanical fumigants could be used, but these had to be compounded (see page 45) according to the elemental type of the incubus involved.

Species of Demons

Six types of demon were recognized by the medieval church, but the first of these, the fiery sort, was too elevated to trouble humans. Aerial demons were thought to inhabit the air, and by increasing the density of their bodies could sometimes appear to men. Their specialty was the creation of damaging storms. Terrestrial devils lived in woods, where they set traps for hunters, or in fields, where they led nocturnal travelers astray; some lived in caves, and others, probably the worst kind, lived "in secret with men." Subterranean demons lived in caves in the mountains, and caused earthquakes, winds and fires; they were especially troublesome to miners. Aqueous demons lived underwater in rivers, streams and lakes; they raised storms, sank ships, and killed life in the water. Perhaps because they generally inhabited

mental materials—the eucharistic bread and wine, the oil of extreme unction—were much prized for this kind of magic, and had to be kept securely locked away.

Witches and their demons could make men sterile or impotent and women barren. Female demons who imposed themselves sexually on sleeping men were greatly feared (or were said to be), and much anecdotal evidence was circulated regarding these succubi. Women were also frequently disturbed by comparable demons in male form, known as incubi. St. Bernard managed to preserve a soft, humid places, and were of a restless, turbulent, deceitful and angry character, they were often depicted as women, though they could also appear as men. Finally, there were the lucifugous demons, who fled from light. Appearing only by night, they were greatly to be feared, for, according to Francesco Maria Guazzo's *Handbook of Witches (Compendium Maleficarum*, 1608):

"This kind of demons is altogether inscrutable and of a nature beyond human understanding, being all dark within and shaken with icy passions; malicious, restless and perturbed; and when they meet men at night they vio-

LAMIA

The Latin Vulgate translation of the Masoretic Hebrew Bible by St. Jerome, which was undertaken with the help of rabbinical scholars in 383-405, and which became the official Roman Catholic version of the Bible, did not hesitate to use classical terms for less familiar rabbinical concepts. Thus the female demon known to Jewish commentators as Lilith appears in the Vulgate at Isaiah 34:15, as *Lamia*, a better-known Greek demoness. She was a queen of Libya, whose beauty captivated the god Zeus and infuriated the goddess Hera. Hera killed Lamia's children, and Lamia, mad with grief and envy, took to stealing other women's children, drinking their blood, and murdering them. In time she became ugly, like a hairy animal, a night demon whose name was used to frighten children.

Left: Winged Mélusine, with wimple, flits from an upper window. She was a French fairy, whose nether parts changed into those of a serpent every Saturday. Her husband, Count Raymond, promised faithfully never to visit her on that day, but—perfidious man—broke his word and found out her secret; and so she fled.

FAIRY GODMOTHERS

The story of Cinderella is probably the world's most widespread fairy tale, with origins in China (where small feet were a mark of beauty). In the 345 recorded versions of the story, the Fairy Godmother, a good witch, appears in many forms. In a Scottish version ("Rashin Coatie") she is a little red calf, and in the German version ("Aschenputtel") a white bird, associated with a hazel tree that grows—watered by Cinderella's tears—on her mother's grave.

Above: Cinderella and her fairy godmother.

Opposite: Merlin finds himself enchanted by the witch Nimue (Vivian); illustration by Arthur Rackham for Malory's Morte D'Arthur.

lently oppress them and, with the permission of God, often kill them by some breath or touch….This kind of demons has no dealings with witches; neither can they be kept away by incantations, for they shun the light and voices of men and every sort of noise."

Guazzo records several stories to convince his readers of the reality of the various kinds of demons, and to help with their identification. Here is his account of how an unfortunate French wagoner met with an aerial demon:

"A certain wagoner from Nancy was in a fenny copse on the outskirts of the town of Nancy, cutting wood, when a fierce storm suddenly arose. He made haste towards a cottage to find shelter, and on the way rested under a thick wide-spreading tree, and waited for the storm to abate. There he was surprised to see standing near him another woodman; and when he looked at him more closely (as we do when we meet a stranger) he saw that his nose kept shooting out to the length of a stick and then quickly contracting to its former shape and size; that his feet were cloven hooves; and that his whole body was of immoderate size. He was struck nearly dead with terror at this, and then (as is the Christian custom in difficulties) made the sign of the Cross, after which he found himself alone as before. But he remained so stupefied by his experience that, though he was used to say that he could find his way about Nancy blindfold, now he could not do so even with the most diligent attention; but came to that city with his tongue sticking and his eyes staring and so trembling all over that it was easy to believe what he said had happened. This belief was largely borne out by the report of what some other woodmen had seen at a distance; for they said that it had appeared to them that in that place the air had become thick and wrapped in a dense cloud."

In the popular imagination, as well as in the analysis of the demonologist, spirits were also associated with elements and seasons, though they were not by any means always evil. The French Mélusine, a prototype mermaid, was an evil aqueous demon, but the 14th-century English romance of *Sir Gawain and the Green Knight* has as one of its principal characters a kind of vegetation spirit who lives with a witch (or succubus) but whose principal task (like Satan's in the Old

Right: *Druids harvesting mistletoe with a golden sickle. According to the Roman historian Pliny, Druid priests venerated the plant, provided it was found growing on an oak tree, and harvested it on the sixth day of the moon in the manner shown here. The Druids, Pliny says, believed that a potion made from the plant's juice could make barren animals fertile, and was a protection against all poisons.*

*The parasitic mistletoe (*Viscum album*) is indeed rich in alkaloids, and was widely used in Europe as a protection against witches. Its cut branches turn a golden yellow as they age, lending the plant a numinous quality noted by the Roman poet Vergil, and perhaps responsible for its identification with the Golden Bough. This grew in the grove of the goddess Diana at Nemi, in Italy, and was the plant which the hero Aeneas, at the suggestion of the Cumaean Sibyl, plucked to help him gain access to the underworld.*

Testament) is to test the virtue of knights. In his human guise he appears as the hospitable Sir Bertilak, an addicted hunter, who lives in a splendid castle with an alluring consort called simply "the Lady."

This ravishing temptress, who does her best to seduce the courteous Sir Gawain, is accompanied by—is perhaps more properly the agent of—another woman, elderly and of a grand manner, wrapped in fine silks but repulsive:

"Nothing was bare on that beldame but the black brows,
The two eyes, protruding nose and stark lips,
And those were a sorry sight and exceedingly bleary:
A grand lady, God knows, of greatness in the world, well tried!
Her body was stumpy and squat,
Her buttock bulging and wide;
More pleasure a man could plot
With the sweet one at her side."

This crone, though not named, is undoubtedly the witch Morgan le Fay, whose special preoccupation was to test the chastity of King Arthur's knights; she built a chapel in a valley, from which

A HARD VIEW OF ADAM

From the early miracle play *The Mystery of Adam*

Devil: Adam I've seen, but he's too rough.
Eve: A little hard!
Devil: He'll soon be soft enough!
  Harde than Hell he is till now.
Eve: He's very frank!
Devil: Say very low!
  To help himself he does not care;
  the helping you shall be my share
  For you are tender, gentle, true,
  The rose is not so fresh as you;
  Whiter than crystal, or than snow that falls from heaven
    on ice below.
  A sorry mixture God has brewed, you too tender,
    he too rude.
  But you have much the greater sense.
  Your will is all intelligence
  Therefore it is I turn to you.
  I want to tell you—
Eve: Do it now!

Adam later whines:

  The woman that you made me take
  First led me into this mistake.
  She gave the apple that I ate
  And brought me to this evil state.
  Badly for me it turned, I own,
  But all the fault is her's alone.

no unchaste knight could ever escape, and this is presumably the prototype of the barrow-like Green Chapel in Sir Gawain. She is also strongly associated with water, being connected with the Celtic goddess Matrona, from whom the name of the River Marne is derived. In Brittany, the fishermen called the mermaids who sometimes lured them to watery graves "Morgans."

Morgan le Fay is thus a demon of the aqueous kind. She is also the opponent and conqueror of the magician Merlin, who was born at Carmarthen in Wales as the offspring of an incubus and a nun. It was he who set Arthur the task of removing the sword from the stone, who magically transported Stonehenge from Ireland to England, and who, in some of the many versions of his legend, is the begetter of the Anti-Christ. In general, though, Merlin is the friend of Arthur and the Knights of the Round Table, a virtuous figure who meets his doom when he falls in love with an emanation of Morgan le Fay, a nymph named Nimue. She succeeds in getting a charm from him, and then uses it to seal him in a rock under a whitethorn tree, or, in another version of the story, in a cave in Merlin's Hill, just outside Carmarthen.

As the coming fires of witch-mania drove out the Celtic mists, it was probably the best place for a wizard to be.

Above: Forbidden fruit, intimately given to a supportive Eve; painting by William Blake, who had his own ideas about good and evil (see chapter seven).

The Years of Fire

Whatever is done for the safety of the State is merciful.
—Sprenger & Kramer, *Malleus Maleficarum*

On or around St. Valentine's Day, 1483, the Devil went to Eisleben in Germany. Posing as a jeweler, and pretending that he was afraid to stay at an inn lest his jewels be stolen, he found lodging with a private family. Before long he managed to seduce the daughter of the house, whose name was Margarita, and then disappeared. In due course—on November 10, 1483, a little more than a year before Pope Innocent VIII inaugurated the high years of the European witch-craze —Margarita produced the Devil's child. She called it Martin, and later married a local man named John Luther. And that is how Martin Luther came into the world...

Or so the Catholic propagandists would have had people believe. Indeed, some demonologists argued that Martin Luther, all by himself, offered convincing proof that demons could father children—for how else could one account for the existence of such an evil being? It was Luther, after all, the former Augustinian priest and scholar, who had fostered Protestantism by objecting to the Church's profitable sale of indulgences, those useful instruments which, for a price, absolved sins; and it was Luther who, taking St. Paul's doctrine of salvation by faith to an extreme, and denying that priests had authority to mediate between man and God, had asserted the principal articles of Protestant belief: the primacy of individual worship and conscience.

And yet in one regard Luther was very much of his opponents' camp. He shared their beliefs about witchcraft, and thought even harmless witches should be burned for making a pact with Satan. Fellow Lutherans shared his views, and their chief inquisitor, Benedict Carpzov, argued that although torture produced false results, it should still be used, and that even those who merely believed they had attended sabbats (but had not) should be executed, "for the belief implied the will." During a long life this virtuous man read the Bible from cover to cover fifty-three times, took the sacrament every week, and is said to have "procured the death of 20,000 persons."

How did such mortal enemies as

Below: Pope Innocent VIII, in a portrait made in 1484, the year in which he wrote the Bull launching the European witch-craze. His papacy was criticized for its worldliness by Savonarola, the reforming Dominican who earned a noose for taking the same tack with Innocent's successor, Alexander VI.

Protestants and Papists find common ground in Europe's burning-fields? Institutionally, both acted within a matrix whose axes were political fear and ambition. Within that context they shared, despite their other differences, a religious tradition that offered ample textual grounds for, and placed no restrictions against, the pathology of their witchfinding aggression and misogyny. Personally, the agents of witch-mania were a mixed lot. Some were profoundly self-righteous scholars, who felt the heavy burden of the task they undertook for God, Church and state. Some were thieves, and others merely opportunists and cowards, gullible or cynical as their wit permitted. All had the taint, and many the high stink, of sadism. They all, without exception and by definition, lacked compassion, save such as might be defined in the far reaches of an abstract and preposterous theodicy. Above all, they were men, and of their times; in the interim, male behavior has not greatly changed.

God's Storm-troops

On December 9, 1484, Pope Innocent VIII issued the Bull *Summis desiderantibus*, approving a prompt move by two German

INNOCENTIVS·VIII·PAPA·GENVENSIS·
fu fatto del 1484 uise ani 7 mesi o giorni 11

inquisitors against a horrific list of satanic crimes. It had lately come to his ears, the Pope began, that in northern Germany, many persons, of both sexes,

"...unmindful of their own salvation and straying from the Catholic Faith, have abandoned themselves to incubi and succubi, and by their incantations, spells, conjurations and other accursed charms and crafts, enormities and horrid offenses, have slain infants yet in the mother's womb, also the offspring of cattle, have blasted the produce of the earth, the grapes of the vine, the fruits of trees, nay, men and women, beasts of burthen, herd beasts as well as animals of other kinds, vineyards, orchards, meadows, pastureland, corn, wheat and all other cereals; these wretches furthermore torment men and women, beasts of burthen, herd beasts as well as animals of other kinds, with terrible and piteous pains, both internal and external; they hinder men from performing the sexual act and women from conceiving...over and above this they blasphemously renounce the faith which is theirs by the sacrament of baptism, and at the instigation of the enemy of mankind they do not shrink from committing and perpetrating the foulest abominations and filthiest excesses to the deadly peril of their own souls, whereby they outrage the Divine Majesty and are a cause of scandal and danger to very many....

Wherefore We...decree and enjoin that the aforesaid Inquisitors [James Sprenger and Henry Kramer] be empowered to proceed to the just correction, imprisonment and punishment of any persons, without let or hindrance..."

Within a short time Sprenger and Kramer had rushed into print what became the standard witch-hunter's manual, the *Malleus Maleficarum (The Hammer of Witches)*. It surveyed the literature of demonology and witchcraft and suggested guidelines for prosecutors. Remembering their Papal brief to proceed "without let or hindrance," the two

Left: *During the years of witch-mania Europe's civil and ecclesiastical authorities attained perfections of inhumanity while trumpeting their own virtue. This picture of a procedure employed innumerable thousands of times, emphasizes that humiliation was a crucial tactic of the torturers, hand-in-hand with inflicting pain. It is captioned: "You are going to be tortured so much the sun will shine through your body!"*

Dominicans outlined strategies for the use of torture and lies. The inquisitor should get his officers to bind the woman, and "apply to her some engine of torture." But this should be done with an appearance of regret and unwillingness, and before long someone should earnestly ask that the woman be released. At this point the inquisitor can usefully promise the witch her life, providing she gives evidence leading to the conviction of other witches. She will not, of course, escape with her life, but on this count the judge can ease his conscience by discharging himself from the case and deputing another judge to pass the death sentence.

Sprenger and Kramer were aware that torturing a witch was dangerous work, and were careful to provide their students with safety tips. It was necessary, for instance, to strip the witch naked and shave the hair "from every part of her body." This was because witches "in order to preserve their power of silence...are in the habit of hiding some superstitious object in their clothes or in their hair, or even in the most secret parts of their bodies, which must not be named." During his probing search the inquisitor must be watchful not only for demonic charms but for "witch's marks," that is, for any physical blemish that have been placed there by the Devil. Thus any birthmark, wart or mole might provide him with damning evidence of a satanic pact.

After being tortured, given false promises, and minutely inspected in every part of her shaved and naked body, this dangerous woman was to be taken to her cell and given plenty of food and water. Then it was best to let her associate with "honest persons who are under no suspicion." They should chat with her informally, and then

"...advise her in confidence to confess the truth, promising that the Judge will be merciful to her and that they will intercede for her. And finally let the judge come in and promise that he will be merciful, with the mental reservation that he will be merciful to himself or the State; for whatever is done for the safety of the State is merciful."

Below: The Church's propagandists equated heretics with witches, and specialized in proving their bestiality, as in this miniature depicting Waldenses worshipping a goat. The same propagandists apparently saw no bestiality in the witchfinders' use of red-hot irons and bone-crushing instruments.

For the Safety of the State

By the last decades of the 15th century the Catholic Church, with ample reasons to fear for its authority, turned for reassurance to a promising, though not yet fully mature, tradition of ecclesiastical murder.

The first broad hint of the Church's troubles came, perhaps, around 1176, when a wealthy merchant from Lyons, Peter Waldo, gave away his money and preached apostolic poverty as a road to salvation. His followers, who became known as Waldenses, began to preach, and for their advocacy of a poverty quite uncongenial to the clerics, and their impudence in preaching without sanction, they were excommunicated, first in 1184 and again in 1215. Unchastened, they went still further: declaring the supremacy of the Bible, they rejected the sacraments, the sale of indulgences, and—even—Papal authority.

At about the same time, an ancient heresy, perhaps the most difficult of all heresies for the Church to rebut, was resurgent. This was Manicheanism, a creed which St. Augustine himself had once embraced, and which explained Good and Evil as powers warring in a battle whose outcome could not be predicted. Propounded by the philosopher Mani, and mixed with such elements of Gnosticism as the belief that Christ only appeared to have a human body, it had spread from the east, and by the 13th century had made inroads in the southern French district around Albi. Although not Christians, the Albigensians were declared heretics, and in 1208 a ferocious crusade was launched against them. In 1233 Pope Innocent III established the first Inquisition, a system for the legal

investigation of Albigensian crimes, and put the Dominicans, who were named for St. Dominic, but were popularly considered the *Domini canes*—the hounds of God—in charge of it.

A third insult to Papal authority came from the Yorkshire-born priest and scholar John Wyclif, who championed the people against clerical abuses, declared the primacy of the Bible over priestcraft, and inaugurated its translation from Latin into English. He was declared a heretic in 1380 and again in 1382, but was allowed to live out his life without persecution. His followers, known as Lollards, were less fortunate. They condemned the celibacy of monks and nuns as unnatural, denied the doctrine of transubstantiation, were contemptuous of sacraments, prayers for the dead and the efficacy of official confession. They elevated individual conscience, and abjured all war—a doctrine not calculated to assure a steady supply of foot-soldiers to God's monarchs. In 1417, at the direction of King Henry IV, the statute *De Haeretico Comburendo (On the Burning of Heretics)* was established. Few Lollards were actually burned, but a second wave of suppression in 1431 drove the movement underground, and in that fashion it survived until the 16th century.

In Bohemia (now the Czech Republic) Wyclif's ideas, and his own observations of clerical abuse, inspired John Hus to similar views. He not only opposed the suppression of Wyclif's writings, but translated his *Triologus* into Czech; he denied that an immoral Pope could worthily fulfill his duties, opposed the sale of indulgences, and thought that in cases of gross abuse the Church should be subject to civil supervision. In 1410 he was declared heretical, but enjoyed the protection of King Wenceslaus. In 1414 he was given a safe conduct to attend the Council of Constance in Switzerland, but this was ignored and he was arrested there and tried as a heretic. He refused to recant those points which his inquisitors failed to convince him were hereti-

Left: *1517: Martin Luther nailing his 95 theses protesting corruption in the Catholic Church to the door of Wittenberg castle church. In 1518 he was forced—in a public debate with Johann Eck, a theologian famous for his dialectical skill and grasp of canon law—to admit that his views were opposed to those of the Church. Eck obtained a Papal Bull condemning Luther, whose response was to publicly burn the Bull, and in 1521 he was excommunicated.*

Opposite:
St. Augustine, *by Master Gross of Gmaln. This most readable of the Church fathers (354–450) began life as a loose-living heretic but became, after St. Paul, a formidable theologian, helping to establish the Roman Church's doctrines of grace and apostolic succession.*

Left: *St. Dominic (1170?–1220), founder of the inquisitorial Dominican order, is shown burning heretical books in this painting by Pedro Berruguete.*

JOAN OF ARC

By 1412 the course of the Hundred Years' War between France and England had swung decisively in England's favor, and in the village of Domrémy, southwest of Nancy on the Meuse river, Joan of Arc was born into a poor farmer's family. When she was thirteen or so years old she began to hear mysterious voices, which gave her good but simple advice, such as "Be a good girl and go to Church!" The voices were accompanied by a sensation of bright light, and soon she began to see visions of St. Michael, St. Catherine and St. Margaret. They directed her to seek an audience with the Dauphin, whose coronation as King of France had been prevented by the English occupation. And so this illiterate peasant girl set out, and on her way impressed Robert de Baudricourt, the Captain of the French troops at Vaucouleurs, sufficiently for him to help her obtain a royal audience.

She met the Dauphin and impressed him (in part by repeating aloud a prayer he was saying mentally, and by clairvoyantly discovering a sword behind the altar in the Church of Fierbois) so much that she was soon, in male dress, helping to lead a force of 6,000 men to relieve the siege of Orléans. In May 1429, after two weeks of fierce fighting, the siege was lifted. Three months later at Rheims the Dauphin was crowned Charles VII of France, with Joan beside him.

Joan's success at Orléans was followed by victories against English posts along the Loire and at the battle of Patany. She then set out to relieve the siege of Paris, but failing there, turned north to rescue Compiégne. There she was captured by Burgundian troops and sold to their English allies. After spending a year in the dungeons of Rouen she was brought before an ecclesiastical court and charged with the heresy of witchcraft, most seriously with claiming to have direct contact with God. She held her own with the wily doctors of the Church, but was found guilty, as the political situation required. On being given over to the secular authorities she recanted, but soon withdrew her recantation and, on May 30, 1431, was burned at the stake. Her last word, as the smoke engulfed her, was "Jesus," and an English soldier is said to have muttered "We are lost— we have burned a saint!"

Joan's judges did not survive her by long, and the war did indeed soon begin to turn against England, which in 1450 was forced to relinquish most of its French conquests. Joan was beatified in 1909 and canonized in 1920, but debate about the Maid of Orléans and the source of her voices and visions is one without a solution, and is summed up in the following anecdote:

Man of Science: Come with me to Saltpétrière [a hospital with mental patients], and I'll show you twenty Joan of Arcs.
Priest: Has one of them given us back Alsace and Lorraine?

cal, and denied that he had ever held a number of the beliefs ascribed to him, including various of Wyclif's propositions. In 1415 he died heroically at the stake, condemned in part for beliefs his judges knew he had never held.

After his death the Hussites split into two camps, the more radical of which continued their opposition to Papal abuse. These Taborites (named for the castle to which Hus had retreated after being condemned for heresy) went beyond Hus in denying the real presence of Christ in the sacraments, decrying the veneration of saints, and abominably seeking to replace feudalism with a classless society. In 1434 they were defeated at the battle of Lipany by an alliance of more moderate Hussites, known as Ultraquists, and Papal forces. But neither the ideas of the reformers nor the abuses that inspired them came to an end. In 1517—100 years after Lollardy was declared a burnable offense—Martin Luther nailed his 95 Theses to the door of Wittenberg castle church. Later, when the Protestant revolution was accomplished, he would acknowledge his debt to John Hus in the preface to his *Confession of Faith*:

"For indeed, while I was yet a Papist, I was for long a most fervent emulator of the Roman traditions. (The Papists of our times who write against us, are not as serious as I was, but are wholly cold, and are motivated either by hatred or by the desire for profit; they would do the same against the Papists if they could expect from us greater profit or glory.) But while I was a Papist I hated the Picard Brethren sincerely and from my heart, out of a great zeal for God and religion, and not on account of desire for lucre or glory. For when by chance I came upon some books of John Hus, and found them to be powerful, and in accordance with the pure word of God, I began to feel terrified why the Pope and the Council had burned such and so great a man. Terror-stricken I closed the book, fearing that with the honey there might lurk poison by which my simplicity might be infected. So violently had the name of the Pope and Council fascinated me!

But when it pleased Him who had separated me from my mother's womb to reveal to me that son of perdition... searching out all whom the Pope had condemned and put to death as heretics, I praised them as saints and martyrs."

But he did not praise quite all those condemned as heretics. As the Counter-Reformation unfurled its banners, and the reformers themselves split into quarreling camps, the Protestants yielded nothing in the piety of their witch-burning to "that son of perdition," the Pope, and his troops.

The Victims

There seems to have been no limit to the suffering imposed by religious and political zealots during the aftermath of the Reformation. Lutherans, for instance, were bitterly opposed to Anabaptists on the question of whether baptism should be conferred on children (as they thought) or only on those old enough to understand it (as the Anabaptists believed). The city of Muenster, an Anabaptist stronghold, was ruled during the last phase of its siege by Lutheran forces, by John Bockelson of Leiden, a 26-year-old prophet and self-styled King-Elect of the World. In 1535 he issued a number of edicts, including these:

Polygamy to be the rule. This was promulgated after Bockelson was discovered in adultery. In devout conformity with his own ruling, he took sixteen wives and a large number of concubines. Those objecting to his edict were to be beheaded, and four women who refused to take additional husbands were accordingly executed in a single day. The executioner, Knipperdolling, beheaded his own wife when she tried to escape from the city. "The father irresistibly prompted me to do this," he explained. When one of Bockelson's "Queens" won-

Opposite: *The burning of St. Joan of Arc. When her clothes had been burned off, the executioner doused the fire a little, allowing the crowd in Rouen's Old Market Place to observe the nakedness of the twenty-two-year-old virgin, unobscured by smoke. When she was dead, and the crowd well satisfied, a huge fire was built to reduce her body and bones to ashes, lest Christendom still be afflicted by the evil she had contained, or the English war effort hampered by relics able to stir the French resistance.*

Above: *A 13th-century illumination of book burning. The Roman Catholic Church published its last edition of the famous* Index Librorum Prohibitorum *(Index of Banned Books) in 1948, and withdrew the associated penalty of excommunication in 1966.*

Right: *A revealing woodcut from a book about Scotland's North Berwick witch trials (1590–91): members of the weaker sex hasten to hand their children to Satan, faithless even to biological imperatives and social duty, and heedless of the awful things flying above them.*

dered if it could be proper that she and her husband's entourage should gorge themselves while others in the city had nothing to eat but leather, candles and corpses, he personally executed her; and then danced on her corpse, shouting *"Gloria in excelsis!"*
Polyandry (a woman's taking more than one husband) *to be a capital offense.*
All girls over 12 to be forced to marry.
Theft to be a capital offense.

A ten-year-old girl was executed for stealing a turnip.

When Muenster fell, Bockelson, Knipperdolling and one Bernard Krechting were paraded through the country in chains for six months. Then, on January 12, 1536, they were returned to Muenster and, in front of a large crowd, were tortured with red hot pincers and finally dispatched with a red-hot dagger. The crowd was said to have been un-nerved—to have had its holiday mood spoiled—by Bockelson's shrieks of agony, and by the smell of roast flesh, which filled the market place. As a final mark of disfavor, the bodies of the three men were hanged in iron cages from the tower of St. Lambert's Church.

Children

Though the witchfinder's power was virtually unlimited, his lot was not a happy one. However unflinching he was in applying torture, however unremitting in his prosecutions and burnings, the number of witches increased. With every confession there came (because he demanded them) the names of yet more witches to be examined, and with those examinations still more names. And so, after years of devoted work, even a prince among witchfinders must be discouraged; must wonder if more might not have been done: if some small refinement of cruelty or enthusiasm, some trifling increase of sternness, might not have improved his results.

Even Nicolas Remy, Procurer General for Lorraine from 1591–1606, who earned the title "Scourge of Witches" by dispatching 900 persons during that period (a respectable fifteen-year average of five witches a month) was troubled by self-doubt, if not self-loathing, on the grounds of his undue tenderness towards children. Although he followed custom in sentencing the many children who had been "led away at a tender age by their parents to sin" to nothing more serious than being stripped naked and whipped while they watched their parent(s) being burned to death, he had "never thought that the law was fully satisfied by such methods." He did sentence an incorrigible sixteen-year-old to be crucified for theft (the boy had, after all, ignored three whippings and one branding), but that

was hardly a compensation. In Wurzburg 300 children, some as young as three and four, confessed to sexual intercourse with demons, and many considered the seven-year-old minimum age for execution absurdly lenient.

One who did was Henri Boguet, a jurist who condemned 600 persons to death and personally supervised the torture of an eight-year-old girl. He cited the ancient law of *Excipiuntur* as precedent: a child below the age of puberty who was not moved to tears by its master's death was thereby guilty of a capital offense. And there was always Yahweh's inspiring example: he had summoned two bears to eat forty-two children for laughing at Elisha's baldness.

Even when a decree was passed, as it was in the Castellany of Bouchain, Hainault, protecting girls of less than twelve from execution, the law knew how to be patient. Anne Hauldecoeur was barely seven when she was imprisoned for witchcraft by the Lieutenant of Bouchain, Charles van der Camere. She spent the next five years in jail, and on her twelfth birthday, July 11, 1619, was promptly taken out and executed.

And if children were not whipped or executed they were often used by the authorities as informers and finger-pointers, as happened in England's famous Lancashire Witch Trials of 1612. In that case, Elizabeth Sowthern, a blind beggar in her eighties, was examined by magistrates in the wake of gossip that she was a witch (a miller's daughter had died a year after his testy encounter with the old woman). Shamefully weak in the face of judicial pressure, she soon admitted that she had indeed killed the miller's daughter, with the aid of her imp Tibb, and implicated her granddaughter Alison, and another octogenarian beggar, Mrs. Anne Whittle, "a very old withered spent and decreped creature." Alison, eleven years old, confessed to using "her devilish art of witchcraft" to lame a peddler who had refused to open a packet of pins for her, and Mrs. Whittle confessed to murdering one Robert Nutter of Pendle

Forest by witchcraft. Her daughter, Anne Redfearne, and Mrs. Sowthern's daughter Elizabeth Device (Alison's mother) were also charged in Nutter's murder.

Then two things happened. First, a rumor reached the ears of Justice Nowell that eighteen women and two or three men had met at Mrs. Sowthern's house and, at a Sabbat supper, had plotted to free the witches. They were going to kill the jailer and blow up Lancaster Castle, in whose dungeons the women were being held. Nine of the conspirators were arrested, the others escaped. Next, Jannet

Above: Saturn Devouring his Young, *by Goya. As Time insatiably devours his children, so the witch-crazy Church devoured those in whom its social, theological, and political strategies had bred poverty's discontent and inquiry's disobedience.*

Above: *1608: A woodcut from Brother Francesco-Maria Guazzo's sex-and-violence-soaked best-seller,* Compendium Maleficarum, *shows witches in the act of roasting the corpse of a child, prior to using it in a potion.*

Right: *Convicted in the Lancashire Witch Trials of the offense, but not the felony, of witchcraft (she killed a horse, not a human) Margaret Pearson was sentenced to "stand upon the Pillarie in open Market at Clitheroe, Paddiham, Whalley, and Lancaster, foure Market dayes, with a Paper upon your head, in great Letters, declaring your offence...," then to spend a year in jail.*

and James Device, Elizabeth's other children, informed the authorities that their mother had a brown dog called Ball, and that she used it to murder people. Then Jannet, nine years old, revealed that James, twenty-ish and simple-minded, had a dog too, Dandy, and used him for the same purpose. Off to jail with brother James, a patent witch.

At this point, enter Alice Nutter, mistress of Roughlee Hall. She was a wealthy woman, "of good temper, free from malice and envy." She was also one of the bomb-plotters, young Jannet declared. So off to jail with Mrs. Nutter. She was charged, along with Mrs. Sowthern and her daughter Elizabeth, of the murder by witchcraft of one Henry Mitton, and a powerful motive was established: she had done it because Mitton had rebuffed Mrs. Sowthern's request for a penny.

Anne was acquitted of the murder of Robert Nutter (Jannet being not fully competent, the authorities may have felt, to offer convincing testimony about a murder that occurred some nine years before she was born). The mob howled. In the bulldog spirit of English justice, Anne was quickly re-arrested, this time for the murder of Christopher Nutter (Robert's father), and a more satisfactory judgment was reached.

The final score: Elizabeth Sowthern—dead in jail before she could be hanged; Elizabeth, Alison, and James Device—hanged; Anne Whittle and Anne Redfearne—hanged; Alice Nutter—hanged; three others—hanged. (In England, only high treason—a crime against the king—was punishable by burning. Witchcraft, considered "only" a crime against God, carried the lighter penalty of hanging.)

And young Jannet Device? Twenty-two years after the Lancashire Witch Trials, she and several others were accused of witchcraft by little Edmund Robinson, who had a gruesome tale of a Sabbat he'd been taken to. The women were carted off to London to be examined for witch-marks by the King's own doctor. He found nothing, and the women were pardoned. As for Edmund, he admitted he hadn't been to a Sabbat after all; he'd been stealing plums.

Women

If children fared badly in the witchfinding holocaust, women did worse. The primary handbook, the *Malleus Maleficarum*, had reminded the witchfinders of what most right-thinking men already knew from their Bible: that women were intrinsically evil. It was therefore not difficult to prove the guilt of women, and in his *Discours des Sorciers* Henri Boguet (he who tortured little girls) provided judges with a useful outline of the signs indicating a degree of guilt sufficient to warrant torture:

1. If the accused generally turns his eyes to the ground during his examination...
2. If the parents of the accused were witches...
3. If the accused has a mark upon him...
4. If the accused is prone uneasily to fall into a mad and trembling rage and blaspheme and use other execrations...
5. If the accused makes as though to weep, and yet sheds no tears; or even if he only sheds a very few...
6. If the accused has no cross on his rosary; or if the cross is defective in some particular...
7. If the accused has at times been reproached with being a witch, and has let the reproach pass unanswered, without seeking redress...
8. If he asks to be re-baptised...

Sometimes the judges faced an inconvenience in the form of a witness who testified that the accused had been somewhere else at the time of whatever sorcery was in question. But there was a solution, admitted by Judge Matthew Hale at England's Bury St. Edmunds witch trials of 1645. A person might prove s/he was somewhere else at the time of purported witchery, but this was actually no proof: s/he might be said (and was said) to have merely projected a specter as an alibi—and what could be stronger proof of a demonic pact than an ability like that? This useful stratagem was widely employed in the Salem witch trials, as Cotton Mather reported in his *Magnalia*: "...divers were condemned, against whom the chief evidence was founded in the spectral exhibitions."

By following such standards of evidence, and remembering St. Thomas

Aquinas' opinion that a heretic (unlike an infidel) had no legal or other rights, the witchfinders were sometimes able to hold their own against the tide of evil. After the Catholic re-conquests in Germany during the Counter-Reformation, the Prince-Archbishop of Trier, Johan von Schöneburg, and his Suffragan Bishop Peter Binsfeld, proved to be such stalwarts. Between 1587–93 they managed to burn more than 300 people in 22 villages, having previously (in 1585) left two villages with only a single living female inhabitant between them. The children of the condemned were banished, and their property confiscated; officials "looked for wealth in the ashes of the victims," and found it; the executioner dressed in silver and gold.

Above: *The frontispiece to* Discovery of Witches *(1647) by England's Witch Finder General, Matthew Hopkins, a judicial murderer. It depicts the familiars he claimed to have seen visit Elizabeth Clark in her cell after he had kept her awake for four days (orthodox torture being not permitted by English common law). His testimony was accepted, and she was hanged.*

One part of the trouble with women was their way of congregating in Sabbats. The first clue to the existence of these filthy conventions was discovered in the heresies of certain canons of Orléans, who were burned for their beliefs in 1022. In the retrospective account of their mischief, a monk named Jerome revealed that these canons and their female companions met together at night to invoke demons, which appeared to them in the form of animals. When this happened, a maelstrom of fornication took place, the offspring of which were ritually murdered and burned, their ashes being preserved. If anyone tasted these ashes (which were sometimes compounded into forgeries of the Blessed Sacrament), that person was irrevocably bound to the cult. In 1190 Walter Mapes, an English chronicler familiar with French ways, described how at heretical meetings a great black cat—Satan himself—would

make its way down a rope hanging from the ceiling and receive obeisance in the form of an obscene kiss. This detail was elaborated, in a Bull issued in 1233 by Pope Gregory IX, to include Satan's appearance, at heretical gatherings in Germany, as a toad or a "furry man."

Gregory's indignation at these goings on helped set the tone of Europe's subsequent dealings with witches:

"It would not be a sufficient punishment if the whole earth rose against them, if the very stars revealed their iniquities to the whole world, so that not only men but the elements themselves should combine for their destruction and sweep them from the face of the earth, without sparing age or sex, so that they should be in eternal opprobrium to the nations."

In time the main force of this Papal curse, with fire as the principal conspiring element, would fall upon women, and the heretical gatherings would become mainly female conventions at which occurred every kind of abomination the witchfinders could imagine (and their imaginations ranged very wide indeed), along with their victims' own fantasies and whatever scraps of folklore they remembered.

When not oppressed by the inquisitor's enthusiasm, women sometimes described imaginary gatherings that were pagan in tone but quite lacking the dark colors of the demonic Sabbat. This occurred in Sicily, where the Spanish Inquisition (then responsible for that island, and by tradition more interested in the iniquity of Jews than witches) took a relatively tolerant line with the *donas de fuera*—who were a kind of cross between fairies and witches understood in a non-satanic sense—and their fairy tales.

According to Sicilian custom, the fairies were organized into local Companies, and led by a Queen known as *Reina de las Hadas* (Queen of the Fairies), *La Senora Griega* (The Greek Lady), *La Sabia Sibila* (The Wise Sibyl), *La Matrona* and several other names. In

1588 a fisherman's wife in Palermo told the Inquisition that she and her company rode on goats through the air to a country called Benevento, which belonged to the Pope:

"There was a great plain there on which there stood a large tribune with two chairs. On one of them sat a red young man and on the other a beautiful woman...the first time she went there—when she was eight years old—the ensign and other women [sic] in her company said she must kneel and worship this king and queen and do everything they told her, because they could help her and give her wealth, beauty and young men to make love with. And they told her she must not worship God or Our Lady. The ensign made her swear on a book with big letters that she would worship the other two. So she took an oath to worship them, the king as God and the queen as Our Lady, and promised them her body and soul...And after she had worshipped them like this, they set out tables and ate and drank, and after that the men lay with the women and with her and made love to them many times in a short time.

All this seemed to her to be taking place in a dream, for when she awoke she always found herself in bed, naked as when she had gone to rest. But sometimes they called her out before she had gone to bed. In order that her husband and children should not find out, and without going to sleep (as far as she can judge) she started out and arrived fully clothed.

She went on to say that she did not know at that time that it was devilment, until her confessor opened her eyes to her errors and told her that it was the Devil and that she must not do it any more. But in spite of this she went on doing it until two months ago. And she went out joyfully because of the pleasure she took in it...and because they [the king and the queen] gave her remedies for curing the sick so that she could earn a little, for she has always been poor..."

Compared with this, the Sabbat discovered by most inquisitors (which is to say, the description agreed to by most women under torture and in response to leading questions) was a grim thing. The following account, taken from Francesco Maria Guazzo's *Compendium Maleficarum*, published in 1608, contains most of the features the inquisitor's insisted on finding in the Sabbat fiction, simultaneously showed the devotees as depraved to a subhuman degree and as such great dupes that they kept returning to something in which there was much pain and no pleasure. The pinnacle of this invention was achieved in the case of women, who proved their degradation by copulating

Above: "Where is Mama Going?" *Goya's* Caprichos *series. She is going, with the help of her friends, since she is a trifle weightier than when she first took up this kind of thing, to a Sabbat. An owl has a low place on the aerial totem, and a kitty with an umbrella is along for the ride. No painter was more scathing about the witchcraft fantasy than Goya.*

with the Devil, and then confirmed their stupidity by continuing in that relation, despite its being, as they were obliged to affirm, just as painful, repellent and disgusting as most odious fantasies of their yearning inquisitors.

Before witches go to a Sabbat, Guazzo declared, "they anoint themselves upon some part of their bodies with an unguent made from various foul and filthy ingredients, but chiefly from murdered children." They fly to the appointed place upon a stick, a broom, a shovel, a goat, an ox or dog, usually arriving there at about ten p.m., the most propitious hour; at the place there is a fire, and the devil, "in some terrible shape, as of a goat or dog" is seated on a throne. The witches offer him "pitch black candles or infants' navel cords; and kiss him upon the buttocks in sign of homage."

Then the witches sit down at tables to eat food provided by the demons; but "the feasts are all foul either in appearance or in smell, so that they would easily nauseate the most ravenously hungry stomach." Wine is served, but "black, like stale blood, and is given to the feasters in some filthy sort of drinking horn." Some witnesses testified that human flesh was served at the feasts, but there was general agreement that whatever was served, the witches were "just as hungry and thirsty afterwards as they were before."

After the feast (or sometimes before) there was dancing (always in a circle, to the left), but this was a poor affair too, bringing the participants no pleasure but only "labour and fatigue and the greatest toil." After the dancing, copulation with demons was in order, but this was likely to be the biggest let down of the evening. In 1594 (the year in which Shakespeare probably wrote *Romeo & Juliet*) a girl from Aquitaine freely admitted that after being "corrupted at a tender age by a certain Italian" she had accompanied him to a Sabbat, where the Devil had appeared as "a large and perfectly black goat, well-horned." In due course the goat took her off into the woods, and "pressing her against the ground, penetrated her: but the girl said that she found this operation quite lacking in any sensation of pleasure, for she rather experienced a very keen pain and sense of horror of the goat's semen, which was as cold as ice."

This last point, regarding the temperature of the Devil's semen, was a particularly important one for the torturers to extract in "confession." Anxious to prove that copulation with the Devil was a behavior of almost epidemic porportions, they explained the lack of demonic offspring by postulating that the semen was too cold to be generative, and that the Devil could only reproduce by acquiring semen from human men. They further explained the witches' repeated (yet most unpleasing) sex with the Devil as a mark of woman's insatiable lust, that perennial source of male alarm.

The plague of the 14th century had killed up to half of the European population. The Church, as the major landowner and political force, required a renewed supply of serfs and soldiers, and thus became intensely interested in the reproductive capabilities of women. In 1556 the French parliament passed a law requiring all pregnancies to be registered, and all births to be officially witnessed. Once registered, a woman who failed to provide evidence of a live birth faced a capital charge of infanticide. But contraception and abortion were both available in some form or another from midwives, who became high-profile targets of the witchfinders, and they remained so. Reproductive issues continue to pose both moral and religious questions which are deeply controversial.

A BUFFETING FOR THE ASTROLOGERS

From Martin Luther's *Table Talk*:

There are many reasons I can't believe in astrologers... First, the calendars never agree. One astrologer prophesies that it will be warm, another that it will be cold....Second, when a child is born, the rays of all the signs above the horizon are said to reach that child. For the child is, as it were, a poppy seed in comparison with the smallest star. Now, I ask, why is it that all the stars don't affect the child equally if all reach him equally? Third, why does the effect occur outside the uterus, at the very hour and minute when the child comes out of the uterus, and not in the uterus?....Do you mean to suggest that the stars care about a little skin on the woman's belly when otherwise the sun gives life to every member? Fourth, Esau and Jacob were born under one sign and in rapid succession. Where did the diversity of their natures come from? The astrologers rack their brains about this, but they can't offer a solid explanation.

Above: The burning of Urbain Grandier in Loudun, France. He was a philandering priest who died, heroically, to satisfy a few special needs: those of Cardinal Richelieu's bruised ego; of ambitious sycophants; of a few nuns for a handful of cash; and of a town hungry for the tourists brought in by a convent where lewd shows were staged as examples of demonic possession.

A Male Witch

Sometimes even the most farcical rules of evidence were insufficient to snare a victim, and then the authorities resorted to simple lies, bribery and deception. This was so in the famous case of Father Urbain Grandier—one of the relatively few in which a man suffered the penalties of witchcraft—and the possessed nuns of the Ursuline convent at Loudun.

Grandier was a handsome priest in the parish of St.-Pierre-du-Marché in Loudun. Like many priests of the period he was neither chaste nor abstemious, but unlike most his flamboyant refusal to pay lip service to the clerical conventions led to his being charged, in 1630, with immorality. He was suspended from his parochial duties, but within a year, thanks to his connection with the Archbishop of Bordeaux, the ban was lifted. Fearing that Grandier would seek revenge on them,

his enemies then devised a further plan to undo him, and for it enlisted the help of a Father Mignon, confessor at the Ursuline convent in Loudun.

With Mignon's help the convent's Mother Superior, Sister Jeanne des Anges, and another nun were persuaded to claim that Grandier had bewitched them—by the simple but sinister expedient of throwing a bouquet of roses over the convent wall. To prove it, they gave convincingly convulsive performances as women possessed, but the Archbishop was unconvinced and simply ordered Mignon and his co-conspirator, Father Pierre Bauré, to cease their exorcisms.

Now Grandier suffered the consequences of a fateful mistake. He had previously published a satire gravely offensive to Cardinal Richelieu, who, at the time, had been out of royal favor. Now Richelieu was again in control of

France's political affairs, and when an ally of his, Jean de Laubardemont, who was also a relative of Jeanne des Anges, visited Loudun on business, he discovered that one of the nuns was related to Richelieu, and a new plot to punish Grandier was hatched. A commission of compliant local officials was formed, and Grandier was again arrested on charges of witchcraft. With help of Jesuit, Franciscan and Capuchin exorcists the "possessed" nuns were again set in motion, and the charges of Grandier's alleged diabolically obscene behavior were elaborated.

Meanwhile, Grandier did little to protect himself from the case that was being built against him. This was a bad mistake, and on November 30, 1633, he was arrested, jailed, and subjected to a search of his body for witch's marks. These were quickly and falsely found, though two witnesses, an apothecary and a surgeon, observed the fraud. Now Grandier's legal rights were entirely brushed aside by the Cardinal's men. He was denied a trial by a secular court, and instead was given into the hands of an investigating committee which refused to hear the testimony of nuns who now wished to retract their evidence against him—they were clearly inspired to do so by the Devil; even the Mother Superior, who appeared at the trial with a noose round her neck, threatening to kill herself unless she were allowed to retract her evidence, was ignored. A local doctor, who had observed fraud during the supposed exorcisms of the possessed nuns, and who wished to give evidence for Grandier, was ordered by Laubardemont to be arrested, and saved his skin by fleeing to Italy. A public meeting organized on Grandier's behalf was quickly described as a plot against the King, and quashed.

On August 19, 1634, Grandier was found guilty, and condemned to be first tortured and then burned alive. His courage under torture was remarkable: though the marrow oozed out of his broken bone, he refused to falsely incriminate any other person as an accomplice in his imaginary crimes; when he prayed to God, it was explained that the Devil was his God, and when finally he was tied to the stake in Loudun's marketplace, it was said, though there is conflicting evidence, that the friars prevented him from saying any final words by smashing him in the mouth with a heavy crucifix on the pretext of giving it to him to kiss. He was also denied the mercy of being strangled before his body was burned, the garrote being knotted in such a way as to render it ineffective. The fire was lit by a Franciscan Father, who, with de Laubardemont's wife, is said to have taken much pleasure in Grandier's struggles as the flames consumed him.

After his death the nuns of Loudun continued their possessed behavior, bringing many tourists to the town—their displays were said to be more obscene than might be observed in most brothels. Eventually Richelieu lost interest in the case and discontinued the pension that he had been paying to the "demoniacs." The nuns then promptly recovered their senses, the displays stopped, and peace returned again to the house of God.

Below: *Witches at their caldron. In the witchfinder's lexicon the two main stereotypes of Things That Women Do—cooking and raising babies—were turned upside down and made disgusting: they gave their children to the Devil, or ritually murdered them, and when they cooked, the results were a poisonous stew. In their third area of usefulness, sex, women (for all were potential witches) proved themselves incapable of appreciating a good man by placing frigid facsimiles of themselves in the marriage bed while they stole off to couple with demons.*

A small postscript: Father Lactance, who had lit Grandier's pyre, died within a month of the burning, saying "Grandier, I was not responsible for your death." Father Tranquille, the Capuchin exorcist-conspirator, died insane within five years of Grandier's death, and the "witch-pricker," Dr. Mannouri, died in a delirium of guilt. Father Bauré, an agent of the original conspiracy, was banished from France in 1640 for collusion in another case of pretended demonic possession at Chinon. There, investigators found that women supposed themselves possessed solely on his word, and that evidence against a priest accused by Bauré and a female accomplice of raping a woman on the high altar had been faked—the blood was that of a chicken.

Jews

The first major persecution of Jews in Europe occurred during the grim years of the Black Death, when hundreds in Germany were accused of poisoning wells and were burned to death. St. Bernardino, a Franciscan, inflamed Italian mobs against Jews for their usury and for having crucified Christ, and in 1391 his message was taken up in Spain by another Franciscan, St. Vincente Ferrer. In 1492 the Spanish Inquisitor, General Tomas de Torquemada, succeeded in expelling from Spain all Jews who refused to convert to Christianity. Those who did convert then became liable to trial for heresy, an opportunity that did not escape the Inquisitors.

For many inquisitors, Jews and witches were interchangeable scapegoats. Pierre de Lancre, the famous demonologist and inquisitor of Bordeaux and prosecutor of the Basque witches, found both equally hateful. In his *L'Incredulité et mescréance du sortilège pleinement convaincue* (Paris, 1629) he described Jews as poisoners of wells, murderers of Christian children, magicians and werewolves;

they were hated by God for "their filth and stink...their Sabbaths and synagogues," and were duly condemned by him to crawl through the world like snakes. In almost identical language Gougenot des Mousseux, the primary source of modern anti-Semitism, called Jews "the representatives on earth of the spirits of darkness." They were the masters of a cult of evil established by the Devil himself, he wrote in *The Jew, Judaism, and the Judai-isation of the Christian People*, published in 1869. With their allies (Christian heretics, Knights Templars and Freemasons), they worshipped Satan, engaged in sexual orgies, and used the blood of murdered Christian children in their rituals, which were designed to give them control of the world's banks, political parties and printing presses. The same lunacy informed the famous *Protocols of the Elders of Zion*, a forgery first printed in 1905 in a religious tract concerning the Second Coming. Stripped of its religious baggage, the *Protocols* would become formative reading for Adolf Hitler.

THE HEROES

A few men were courageous enough to oppose the witchfinders even when witch-mania was at its height. Most were clerics who, while not denying the reality of the Devil, or even of witchcraft, believed that most witchcraft was delusion, that trial procedures were often flawed, prosecutors venal, and evidence obtained under torture both obscene and unreliable.

One of the first of those who put his life at risk for the sake of his conscience was Johann Weyer (or Weir), a Protestant doctor. He was the personal physician of the Duke of Cleves, without whose protection he would probably have been burned at the stake for his *De Praestigiis Daemonum (Demonic Illusions)*, published in 1563. Although Weyer believed in demons, he was convinced that the witch trials were travesties of justice and humanity, and that evidence obtained by torture was worthless. Sample chap-

ter titles from his book included: *All accounts which confirm the fiction of diabolical intercourse are themselves fictions*; and *Examples of poor innocent women punished because they were suspected of maleficium*.

Another confession is examined, and the point is made that no one can be injured by words or curses. It is also shown that *Lamiae* [witches] are not of sound mind.

With the help of his wife, Weyer took into his own home a girl who, under

Above: *The torturers' workshop; a 16th-century engraving of a confession-factory.*

Right: *Johann Weyer (or Wier) took a sane view of witchcraft, and risked speaking his mind.*

Below: *England's Chelmsford witches, (1589). Much evidence was provided by children, and two boys, politically ahead of their time, were congratulated for turning in their unmarried mothers. Three of the four persons executed, including Joan Prentis, were hanged within two hours of being sentenced.*

supposed demonic influence, had purportedly not eaten for several months. The Weyers observed that the girl was secretly being fed by her sister, but after a few weeks of kindly care, she began to eat normally. Sigmund Freud considered *De Praestigiis* to be one of the ten most significant books of all time. But the killing went on.

The first English writer to pour scorn on those he called "witch mongers" was Oxford drop-out, sometime Member of Parliament, country gentleman and horticulturist Reginald Scot. His first book, *The Hop Garden*, published in 1574, helped make Kent, his home county, England's prime hop-growing area. His second, *The Discoverie of Witchcraft*, published ten years later, infuriated King James I, who called it "damnable" and ordered all copies burned.

Scot was 46 when he published *The*

Joannes Wierus

Discoverie, and probably wrote the book because he had been sickened by the notorious trial and execution of the St. Osyth witches at Chelmsford, Kent, in 1582. His tone was ironic, entirely dismissive of the reality of witchcraft, humorous and angry:

"The fables of Witchcraft have taken so fast hold and deepe root in the heart of man, that fewe or none can (nowadaies) with patience indure the hand and correction of God. For if any adversitie, greefe, sicknesse, losse of children, corne, cattell or libertie happen unto them; by & by they exclaime uppon witches. …what treacherous and faithless dealing, what extreme and intolerable tyranny, what gross and fond [stupid] absurdities, what cankered and spiteful malice, what outrageous and barbarous cruelty…what abominable and devilish inventions, and what flat and plain knavery is practiced against these old women, I will set down the whole order of the Inquisition, to the everlasting, inexcusable, and apparent [obvious] shame of all witch mongers."

IOAN PRENTIS & hir Bid

IACKE

GILL

Scot died, without legal harassment, in 1599. But the killing went on.

Father Cornelius Loos was tortured and imprisoned for his opposition to the German witch trials, and his book *De Vera et Falsa Magia (True and False Sorcery)* was destroyed by the Inquisition. He was born in Holland in 1546, denounced Protestantism while a professor at the Catholic College in Mainz, and took a teaching job at Trier. There he was nauseated by what he saw of the persecution of witches, and protested, by every means available to him, to the civil and ecclesiastical authorities. When they ignored him he wrote *De Vera*, denying that the Devil could take substantial form and deploring both the use of torture and the financial profit the witchfinders often extracted from their victims:

THE BASQUE WITCHES

In the annals of witchcraft there are perhaps no more devout and accomplished sorcerers than those Pierre de Lancre faced in his attempts to root out heresy in the Landes and Basque districts of France in 1609. As his 600-page report of his grueling time there (*Tableau de l'Inconstance des Mauvais Anges—Description of the Inconstancy of Bad Angels*) records, as many as 12,000 witches at a time would gather in Hendaye, a town at the mouth of the Bidassoa river, and on one occasion 100,000 assembled, though in this number there were some phantoms. Sabbat attendance was almost a nightly affair, and in the mountainous Basque country known as La Labourt, these Sabbats often included at least 2,000 children. Sabbats were even sometimes held by day, and the Labourt witches were probably the champion among long-distance flyers—sometimes, he observed, they flew all the way to Newfoundland.

In this climate, even a man as hardworking as de Lancre managed to burn only 600 witches. He explained that not only were the majority of the region's 30,000 or so inhabitants witches, but that he was additionally hampered because even those against whom nothing had been proved preferred—unbelievably—to live under Satan's rule than to see their loved ones hauled off to the stake. And there were nasty scenes when some 5,000 fishermen returned from Newfoundland's waters to find that their wives, daughters, sisters and mothers had been burned alive while they were away. Obviously no theologians, these rough men became a howling mob, demanding, often at dagger-point, the retraction of legally obtained confessions, and sometimes even making it impossible for officials to perform their duty.

Despite these deplorable conditions, de Lancre soldiered on, exposing not only witches but even a serious case of werewolfism. A boy had been given a wolf skin by a dusky man in a wood, and admitted that when he put it on he became a wolf, and ran about killing and eating dogs and children. Unfortunately, judicial obstinacy prevented this young sinner, a thirteen-year-old named Jean Grenier, from being dealt with properly: the judges at Bordeaux refused to burn him "because of his age and imbecility" (children of seven and eight commonly showed more sense than he, they said) and because (shades of godless liberalism) he was malnourished (no bigger than a normal child of ten), abused by his father, abandoned by all, and left to wander by himself in the fields, lacking all instruction in the fear of God. And what punishment did these lenient judges impose? No more than that the boy be confined in a convent for the rest of his life, and be hanged if he left it.

How did it happen that La Labourt suffered such extraordinary infestations? De Lancre had an explanation. The intense poverty and ignorance of the people, especially the women, made them an easy prey to Satan's wiles; but more than that, La Labourt had become a favorite refuge for demons expelled from Japan and the East Indies by Christian Missionaries.

In an even wider perspective, it might be noted that the Basque region was another of those mountainous areas (like the Italian, Swiss and French Alps) where feudalism had never been as fully established as the authorities would have liked. In such regions ancient superstitions died hardest (making it all the more difficult to supplant them with new superstitions), and rural society yielded most stubbornly to urban influence. When authority sought to assert itself in such areas, it naturally met with the greatest affronts, and was therefore compelled to the greatest severities.

THE WITCH WHO GOT AWAY

The following story, told by Ralph, Abbot of Coggeshall (1187–1224), relates an incident in the early persecution of the Manicheans. The events described are said to have taken place in the vicinity of Rheims during the reign of King Louis VII of France (1137–80):

"The Lord William, Archbishop of that city [Rheims] and uncle to King Philip, was riding one day for pastime without the city, attended by his clergy; when one of his clerks, Master Gervase of Tilbury, seeing a maiden walking alone in a vineyard, and impelled by the wanton curiosity of youth, went aside to her....Having saluted her and asked whence she came, and who were her parents, and what she did there alone, having also observed her comeliness for a while, he began at last to address her in courtly fashion and prayed her of love…

'Nay,' replied she, with a simple gesture and a certain gravity in her words, scarce deigning to look at the youth, 'Nay, good youth, God forbid that I should ever be thy leman [sweetheart or mistress] or any other man's; for if I were once thus defiled, and lost my virginity, I should doubtless suffer eternal damnation beyond all help.' Hearing which Master Gervase forthwith knew her for one of this most impious sect of Publicans [Manicheans], who in those days were sought out on every hand and destroyed….

While therefore the clerk aforesaid disputed with the maiden, confuting this answer of her's, then the Archbishop came up and bade them take the girl and bring her with him to the city. Then, when he had addressed her in presence of his clergy, and proposed many texts and reasonable arguments to confute her error, she answered that she herself was not so well-instructed as to refute such weighty objections, but confessed she had a mistress in the city who would easily refute all by her reasonings….

The crone was forthwith sought out by the servants and set before the Archbishop. She, therefore—being assaulted on all sides with texts from Holy Scripture, both by the Archbishop himself and by his clergy, that they might convince her of so heinous an error—yet she, by a certain sinister subtlety of interpretation, so perverted all the texts they cited, that all understood clearly how the Spirit of All Error spake through her mouth. For she replied so easily, with so ready a memory, to all the texts and stories

objected to her, whether from the Old or New Testament, as though she had acquired a knowledge of the whole Scriptures, and had been always practised in answers of this kind; mingling falsehood with truth, and baffling the true explanation of our faith with a certain pernicious understanding. Since therefore the obstinate minds of both women could be recalled neither by fair words nor foul…they were shut up in his prison till the morrow.

On the next day they were again publicly challenged to renounce their errors….Yet they…persisted immovably in the errors they had conceived; wherefore they were unanimously adjudged to the stake. When therefore the fire was already kindled in the city, and they should have been dragged by the serjeants to the penalty to which they had been condemned, then that wicked mistress of error cried aloud: 'O madmen and unjust judges! Think ye to burn me now with your fires? I fear not your doom, nor shudder at the flames ye have prepared.'

With these words she suddenly drew from her bosom a spool of thread, which she cast through a great window of the hall, yet keeping the clue [ball of thread or yarn] in her hand, and crying with a loud voice in all men's hearing 'Catch!' No sooner had she spoken this word than she was caught up from the ground, and followed the ball like a bird through the window, under all men's eyes….But what became of that witch, or whither she was spirited away, no man of that company could discover.

Meanwhile the maiden, who had not yet come to such a pitch of madness in that sect, remained behind. No persuasion of reason, no promise of riches, could recall her from her foolish obstinacy; wherefore she was burned to death, to the admiration [wonder] of many who marked how she uttered no sighs, no tears, no laments, but bore with constancy and cheerfullness all torments of the consuming flames, even as the martyrs of Christ (yet for how different a cause!) who were slain in old times by the heathen in defence of the Christian religion. Petrus Cantor, a father of the Church was well aware that women were abused in this way: 'Moreover, certain honest matrons, refusing to consent to the lasciviousness of priests…have been written by such priests in the book of death, and accused as heretics…while rich heretics were simply blackmailed and suffered to depart.'"

"Wretched creatures are compelled by the severity of the torture to confess things they have never done, and so by cruel butchery innocent lives are taken and by a new alchemy gold and silver coined from human blood."

For his pains, Loos suffered a long imprisonment, was forced to recant, on his knees, before the abominable Peter Binsfeld, Trier's bloodthirsty Suffragan Bishop (whom he had criticized), and was banished. He found work as a curate in Brussels, but despite the danger to his life would not be silent. He was again arrested as a heretic and imprisoned, but—strangely—was released after a few months. He died, his health broken by his imprisonment, on February 3, 1595, at the age of 49. And the killing went on.

Another Catholic priest whose personal experience of the witch trials made him a bitter opponent of the authorities was the Jesuit Father Friedrich von Spee, who served as confessor to those accused of witchcraft. He said that his hair was turned prematurely white by the horror of accompanying so many people he believed were innocent to the stake. His book *Cautio Criminalis (Precautions for Prosecutors)*, published anonymously in 1631, was bitterly critical of the use of torture. When his authorship became known he was transferred to Cologne, and died of the plague before he could be charged as a heretic. In the hundred years following his death the *Cautio* appeared in sixteen editions, and was translated into German, Dutch, French and Polish.

And the killing went on, and on. At the most conservative estimate, 200,000 people were killed in Europe during the witch-hunting years. In their fear of Hell and the Devil, the witch-mongers created a deadly approximation of Hell on earth, as if they might, like magicians, by this simulacrum control the reality they feared.

Overleaf: Execution of a Witch, *by Goya.*

THE WORLD BEWITCHED

Balthasar Beckker (1634–98) published *De Betoverde Weereld (The World Bewitched)* in 1691 in Holland, the only country where translations of Scot's book were permitted. The first two books sold 4,000 copies, the full run, in two months. Though he did not deny the existence of demons, he argued that they could not influence human affairs, and denied the reality of demonic possession; he also asserted that paranormal phenomena should not be explained by witchcraft—such beliefs had crept into Christianity from pagan sources, and should be discounted. He was condemned by Calvinist divines as an atheist, and expelled from the Reformed Dutch Church. The Amsterdam authorities, however, refused to allow the burning of his book by the public executioner, as his opponents demanded.

BALTHASAR BEKKER,

REBECCA LEMP: A VICTIM'S OWN STORY

Among the most moving accounts in all the sad annals of persecution is the correspondence from Rebecca Lemp, jailed in 1590 for witchcraft, to her husband Peter Lemp, a well-educated accountant of Nördlingen, Swabia. The persecutions were promoted here, not by pastors or priests, but by local lawyers, Sebastien Roettinger and Conrad Graf, led by Burgomaster Georg Pheringer. In spite of the favorable testimony of neighbors who took the risk of appearing in their defense, in 1590 thirty-two prominent and well-placed women were burned. Among them were Frau Lemp and the wives of a former burgomaster, a senator, the town clerk, and an important administrator.

The following account, from R. H. Robbins' *Encyclopedia of Witchcraft and Demonology*, includes four documents read in court. The first, a moving letter to Rebecca Lemp from her six young children, was written very soon after her arrest in April, 1590, while her husband was away. The children could not comprehend what was happening and, after a few days, their father still absent on business, wrote to their mother. John, the little scholar of the family, showed off his schooling by signing his name in Latin.

Our dutiful greeting, dearly beloved Mother! We let thee know that we are well. Thou hast informed us that thou art well too. We expect that father will come home today, God willing. So we will let thee know as soon as he gets home. Almighty God grant thee his grace and Holy Spirit that, if it please God, thou mayest come back to us hearty and well. God grant it! Amen.

Dearly beloved Mother, let beer be bought for thee, bread for soup, and little fried fish got, and send to us for a little chicken. I have just killed two. The Rev. Rummel [a friend of the family] has dined with us. If thou needest money, send for it; thou hast some in thy purse. Fare thee well, my beloved Mother; do not be worried about the housekeeping till thou comest back to us. [signed]

Rebecca Lempin, thy loving daughter
Anna Maria Lempin, thy loving daughter
Maria Salome Lempin, thy loving daughter
Joannes Conradus Lempius, *tuus amantissimus filius*
Samuel Lemp, thy loving son
X [mark of Peter Lemp]

For the thousandth time, God grant thee a good night.

The second is Rebecca's letter to her husband: she fears he believes the accusations against her. Naïvely, she tells him not to worry; since she has done nothing wrong, she will not be tortured!

My dearly beloved Husband, be not troubled. Were I to be charged by thousands of accusations, I am innocent, else may all the demons in hell come and tear me to pieces. Were they to pulverize me, cut me in a thousand pieces, I could not confess anything. Therefore do not be alarmed; before my conscience and before my soul I am innocent. Will I be tortured? I don't believe it. Since I am not guilty of anything. Husband mine, if I am guilty of anything, may God reject me forever far from his sight. If they do not believe me, Almighty God, who knows everything, will work a miracle so they will believe me. Otherwise, if I have to stay in this anxiety, there is no God in heaven. Don't hide thy face from me, thou knowest my innocence. In God's name, do not leave me in this anguish which is choking me.

Third is Rebecca's note to her husband, some months later, after she had been tortured five times and had confessed. How she wrote this letter and smuggled it out of jail is not known, but it was intercepted and read in court as evidence of an additional crime, suicide, because she asked her husband to bring her poison.

O thou, the chosen of my heart, must I be parted from thee, though entirely innocent? If so, may God be followed throughout eternity by my reproaches. They force one and make one confess; they have so tortured me, but I am as innocent as God in heaven. If I know the least thing about such matters, may God shut the door of heaven against me! O thou, dearly beloved Husband, my heart is nearly broken! Alas, alas! My poor dear children orphans! Husband, send me something that I may die, or I must expire under the torture; if thou canst not today, do it tomorrow. Write to me directly.—R.L.

[*On the reverse.*] Oh, Husband of thine innocent Rebecca, they take me from thee by force! How can God suffer it? If I am a witch, may God show no pity to me. Oh, what wrong is done me! Why will God not hear me? Send me something, else may I peril even my soul.

The court then dictated a letter which Rebecca had to write to her husband, swearing she had lied and that she was indeed a witch, unworthy of him and her children. Peter Lemp, however, knew his wife too well to be deceived by this ruse, and resolutely replied to the court in the following letter:

Honorable and esteemed lords, most wise and magnanimous! Recently, on June 1, I addressed to the court a humble petition relating to my dear wife, in which I requested that she be set free; but my request was turned down. May my petition this time have a different result. Since then, I have received from my wife a true report, in which she tells me she is closely confined in prison for something of which she is not guilty, and asks me to come to her help—me, her closest, dearest, and best friend, her husband, spouse—and to succor her in her tribulations and suffering. In truth, I would not be a Christian, if I did not seek how to comfort and assist her. [*Peter Lemp then asked for confrontation by witnesses, because he believed the accusations were secured by torture.*] I hope, I believe, I know that during all our life, my wife has never even thought about what she is accused of, let alone having done it. I swear this by my soul. Very many well-respected people, who know me and my wife, testify, as I do, that she has always been a pious, chaste, honest housewife, foe to any evil; that she has always cherished me faithfully as her dear spouse. She has, moreover, as a good mother to her family carefully raised our dear little ones, taught them—together with me—not only their catechism, but furthermore the Holy Bible, especially the beautiful psalms of David. Indeed, thanks to God—and I say this without boasting—all

the children with which God has blessed us, without exception, know and can recite several psalms.

No one in the world—this I say to the best of my belief—can maintain that my wife ever worked the least ill, no matter what, or that anyone had the slightest suspicion about her...

This is why, in my name and in the name of my dear little children, who now number six—God be forever praised—I humbly pray you, for the love of God and the prospect of the last judgment at which Jesus Christ will himself appear as judge, and I beg you, who manifest in yourselves wisdom and duly constituted authority, to show a favorable regard for my dear wife and to set her free.

After it had received this petition of Peter Lemp, the court further tortured Rebecca and condemned her to be burned on September 9, 1590.

Then the witch hunt intensified, and the prisons overflowed. The persecutions ceased only in 1594 when Maria Hollin, who owned the Crown tavern in Nördlingen, maintained her innocence during eleven months in a stinking dungeon, being subjected *fifty-six times* to the most cruel tortures the court could imagine—among the highest number recorded where the victim survived. Its use of torture, the court argued, was actually in the interests of the accused, because it quickly terminated the suspense of uncertainty and indefinite anxiety. Maria Hollin was ultimately rescued by the intervention of Ulm, the city of her birth, which claimed jurisdiction over her. But her resistance at Nördlingen gave courage to Pastor Wilhelm Lutz to speak out in the name of the Protestant churches and, supported by public opinion, force the infuriated lawyers to stop their illegal trials. "The proceedings will never end," preached Lutz, "for there are people who have informed on their mothers-in-law, their wives or husbands, denouncing them as witches. What can come of all this?"

Specters at Salem

You tax me for a wizard. You may as well tax me for a buzzard.
I have done no harm.

— George Jacobs Sr., hanged August 19, 1692,
DESPITE THE WITHDRAWAL OF CHARGES

There are many ways to peer into the future. You can find it prefigured in the coils and colors of a woman's entrails (antinopomancy), in the wrinkles and irregularities of coagulating cheese (tyromancy), in ashes, dates, herbs and stars. Or by dropping hot wax or molten lead—or even the white of an egg—into a glass of water. This last was the form of lekanomancy favored by a few young Puritan girls in Salem Village in the winter of 1692.

They were looking for signs of romance, of fortune, who would they marry, would they be rich. Instead, one of them—not named, but probably nine-year-old Elizabeth Parris, daughter of the Salem Village preacher—saw a coffin in the glass. An unmistakable, spectrally slimy omen of death. But the girls had a taste for the occult, and Reverend Parris had a Caribbean slave, Tituba; in the dark of the winter evenings she told them stories of witchcraft, black, exciting tales of Barbados magic.

Then the excitement got out of hand. Elizabeth and her eleven-year-old cousin, Abigail Williams, who lived in the Parris home, began to have convulsions and fits of sobbing. Their behavior got worse: Abigail would run to the fireplace and throw flaming sticks about the house. Then it began to spread to their companions: to Anne Putnam, 12; to Mary Walcott, 16; to Elizabeth Hubbard, 17; to Susan Sheldon and Elizabeth Booth, both 18; to Mercy Lewis, 19; to Mary Warren, 20.

On February 25 Mary Sibley, Mary Walcott's aunt, asked Tituba and her husband, Indian John, to bake a witch's cake.

It was compounded of meal mixed with the urine of the affected children, and was then fed to the Parris family dog, a supposed familiar of the demons. It worked. The children were able to name those responsible for their distress, and on February 29 warrants were issued for the arrest of Sarah Good, Sarah Osborn and the slave Tituba.

Today, the behavior of the young women—dramatic and alarmingly abnormal as it was—would almost certainly be diagnosed as clinically hysterical. In the diagnosis of the time, the girls were demonically possessed. By summer's end, nineteen of their "oppressors" had been hanged on Witch's Hill, and one man had been pressed to death. Thereafter the name of Salem Village would be forever infamous. The omen of the coffin had been right.

Opposite:
The Accusation *by Howard Pyle. Young hysterics respond on cue to their supposed tormentor; the accused (eyes upcast demurely) protests innocence.*

Below: *A winter evening, and by firelight Tituba entertains Salem's children with tales of magic.*

Right: Cotton Mather had a flair for the uncanny; before the Salem trials began he interviewed a condemned witch and cared for one of her young victims

Below: Mather ministers to Martha Goodwin. As time went by, she recovered her senses.

Supernatural Afflictions

Three years before the Salem girls began to feel themselves afflicted, one of New England's leading ministers had published an account of similar phenomena under the title *Memorable Providences Relating To Witchcrafts And Possessions*. The author, Cotton Mather, son of the famous preacher Increase Mather, had studied medicine and was a member of England's premier scientific association, the Royal Society. He also had considerable journalistic flair, and his book, which was widely read, may be partly credited with helping to create the atmosphere in which the Salem trials took place (though his own attitude towards the events he describes is notably humane). His account also helps explain why the affliction of the Salem girls, who would today be diagnosed as

hysterics, was taken so seriously: it had the hallmarks of something truly supernatural, and their testimony that they were being supernaturally afflicted was accordingly given enormous weight.

In *Memorable Providences* Mather described the case of a young woman named Martha, whose affliction had begun in the summer of 1688. At thirteen she was the eldest daughter of the Goodwin family, and her problems apparently started when some of the family bed-linen went missing. A young laundry girl was suspected, and Martha accused her. The girl's mother, "a scandalous old woman," then defended her daughter and "bestowed very bad language" upon Martha.

The effects, according to Mather, were immediate. Martha began to have "strange fits, beyond those that attend an epilepsy or a catalepsy...." Before long her sister Mercy, aged seven, and her two brothers, Nathaniel, fifteen, and Benjamin, five, began to show the same symptoms. Doctors were called in, but could diagnose no cause but witchcraft. When one of the children began to experience an attack, the others immediately experienced the same symptoms in the

same parts of their bodies. Mather describes these symptoms as follows:

"Sometimes they would be deaf, sometimes dumb, and sometimes blind, and often, all at once. One while their tongues would be drawn down their throats; another-while they would be pull'd out upon their chins, to a prodigious length. They would have their mouths opened unto such a wideness, that their jaws went out of joint; and anon they would clap together again with a force like that of a strong spring-lock. The same would happen to their shoulder-blades, and their elbows, and hand-wrists, and several of their joints. They would at times ly in a bennumed condition; and be drawn together as those that are ty'd neck and heels; and presently be stretched out, yea, drawn backwards, to such a degree it was fear'd the very skin of their bellies would have cracked. They would make most pitteous out-cries, that they were cut with knives, and struck with blows that they could not bear. Their necks would be broken, so that their neck-bone would seem dissolved into them that felt after it; and yet on the sudden, it would become again so stiff that there was no stirring of their heads; yea, their heads would be twisted almost round; and if main force at any time obstructed a dangerous motion which they seem'd to be upon, they would roar exceedingly. Thus they lay some weeks, most pittiful spectacles...."

Once witchcraft had been mentioned the local magistrates brought in the abusive old woman, Mrs. Glover, for examination. She dismally failed the various tests they put to her (when asked if she believed in God, for example, she answered too blasphemously for Mather to print her reply, and her attempts—which were in Irish, her only language—to recite the Lord's Prayer were dismally inept). She was therefore jailed, and the children promptly experienced some relief.

Mrs. Glover's case moved forward. She confessed to witchcraft, and her house was searched. From it were brought into the court "several small images, or puppets, or babies, made of raggs, and stuff't with goat's hair and other such ingredients." Mrs. Glover admitted that she used these to torment her victims, which she had accomplished by spitting

BADOUREAU.

Below: *A 19th-century hysterical patient exhibiting the same convulsions as some of Salem's "afflicted."*

Overleaf:
The Damnation of the Young; *altarpiece panel from the Marienkirche, Danzig, by Hans Memling (1433-94). Infant damnation was a common topic for Puritan children, and most were familiar with Michael Wigglesworth's long poem "The Day of Doom," published in 1662. It contains the following plea to God from a child who has died too young to sin; referring to the Adam's Original Sin, he says:*
"Not we but he ate
 of the tree
Whose fruit was
 interdicted:
Yet on us all of his
 sad fall
The punishment's
 inflicted."
(God gives this comforting reply:)
"...every sin's a
 crime.
A crime it is, therefore in bliss
you may not hope to
 dwell,
But unto you I shall
 allow
the easiest room in
 hell."

on her finger and rubbing the chosen doll with it. The afflicted Goodwin children were in court, and when "the vile woman" was given one the dolls, one of the children fell into a fit. The justices repeated the experiment and obtained the same result.

Mrs. Glover was now asked if she had anyone to stand by her, and she said she had. Then, looking into the air, she said, "No, he's gone." That night she was heard in her cell berating the Devil for deserting her. She was next questioned by six doctors, in an effort to determine whether or not she was sane. "Diverse hours did they spend with her; and in all that while no discourse came from her but what was pertinent and agreeable...." The doctors concluded that Mrs. Glover was sane, and she was condemned to death. Mather visited her in the death cell, asked her about her demons, and urged her to repent, all with little effect. On her way to the gallows she said that the children would not be relieved by her death, because others were involved, naming "one among the rest, whom it might be thought natural affection would have advised the concealing of"—presumably her daughter, though Mather makes no surmise.

Mrs. Glover's prediction proved correct. The children continued "in their furnace as before, and it grew rather seven times hotter than it was." They began to bark at each other like dogs, or purr like cats, and to complain of intense heat and cold. Sometimes their limbs seemed to be made of rubber, and sometimes the boy said that his head was nailed to the floor, and then "it was as much as a strong man could do to pull it up." But the children's worst agony occurred when preachers were brought to them. When these ministers "bestowed some gracious counsils on the boy" he immediately went stone deaf; when they prayed or read the Bible, "this would occasion a very terrible vexation to them: they would then stop their own ears with their own hands; and roar, and shriek, and holla, to drown the voice of devotion."

In kindness, and curiosity, Mather took the afflicted girl Martha into his own home, and there her maladies continued unabated. She complained that she was sometimes painfully chained by her unseen assailants; once she tried to dive through the floorboards, saying that "They" had told her there was (silver) "plate" at the bottom of the well. The Mathers inquired of the person from whom they had recently bought the house and discovered that there was indeed a rumor of silver plate at the bottom of the well. Mather experimented to see what sort of books Martha could and could not read. She easily read a book that "pretended" to prove there were no witches; but one which sought to prove the reverse, she could not read at all. If she could be got into Mather's upstairs study, she experienced some relief from her afflictions, but to get her there was always a great struggle, and Mather was "loth to make a charm of the room"—he feared to use it because of the supernatural effects it appeared to cause.

Below: "There They Go!" *A sporting observation by skeptical witch-fancier Francisco de Goya, from his* Capricho *series. When hints of aerial fun and sabbat games were leaked to Salem's witchfinders, they smelled conspiracy, and stepped up their inquiries.*

A day came when Martha announced that on the following day her afflictions would cease, and that she was now able to tell Mather the names of those who had been afflicting her. She did so, but Mather did not publish them or, apparently, inform the authorities. Martha's afflictions eased for a time, returned with great ferocity one weekend, and then eventually disappeared. Her young brother continued to be seriously troubled, but in time his afflictions also disappeared.

Martha Goodwin and the Salem girls were seen as victims of demonic assault, but in a different place and at a different time their behavior might have been given a different interpretation and led in a quite different direction. This did in fact happen, forty-two years after the

Salem outbreak, in the small Massachusetts community of Northampton. There the "afflictions" of the young girls were given another interpretation altogether by the town's soon-to-be-famous minister, Jonathan Edwards. In his view, the moaning and thrashing about of the young women was the painful but hopeful sign of a religious rebirth. By guiding and cultivating the girls' behavior in the light of that interpretation, and with the firm support of the adult community, Northampton produced not witches and hangings, but "a great awakening," a spiritual revival in which adults also shared.

The difference in outcome lay not entirely in the passage of time or even in the character of the officials involved, but in the history and character of the two communities. Northampton was relatively peaceful, Salem Village was not—was famous, rather, for its quarrels and factions, which, within its narrow bounds, echoed faintly Europe's ructions during the years of witch-mania.

Specters and Accusations

When the first of Salem's accused women appeared in court they were examined by two magistrates, John Hathorne and Jonathan Corwin. Sarah Good's husband testified that she was either a witch, or would soon be one, and her four-year-old daughter Dorcas said her mother had familiars: three birds, one yellow and one black, which "hurt the children and afflicted persons." Mrs. Good in turn accused Sarah Osborn. Magistrate Hathorne led the questioning, not in a manner of impartial inquiry, but in the style of a prosecuting attorney, and his questions—"Sarah Good, what evil spirit have you familiarity with?"—clearly assumed his respondent's guilt.

The afflicted perons were present in court, and were asked to say whether Sarah Good was one of those who afflicted them. She was, they said, and immediately fell into fits. When they recovered they revealed that although

Left: *Grim familiar: reports of familiars at Salem featured small birds and a hairy two-footer with a long nose, who enjoyed warming his backside at the kitchen fire. Not all were as manageable, as suggested by this specimen with massive claws and muscular tail, leashed for a stroll, dark with menace.*

Sarah Good was physically removed from them, she had come "spectrally" and tormented them. Mrs. Good protested, scornfully, that she had not. The same procedure was repeated with Sarah Osborn, and "spectral evidence," which was to be a major feature of the subsequent trials, was admitted.

Then Tituba came to the stand. She quickly admitted that she knew the Devil: he was a tall man in black, with white hair, but sometimes he appeared as an animal. He had bidden her do his will, and she had made her mark of agreement in red in a book that had nine names in it. She had seen Sarah Good's and Sarah Osborn's marks there, and in any case she sometimes saw them in the Devil's company, along with two Boston witches whose names Tituba didn't know. Sarah Good's familiars were a cat and a yellow bird, which sucked her between her fingers. Sarah Osborn's familiar had wings, two legs and a head like a woman; she also had another familiar, a hairy creature with a long nose, about two or three feet high; it walked upright like a man, and Tituba had seen it standing by the fireplace in the Reverend Parris's house just the previous night. Sometimes the women rode together through the air on a stick, looking for children to persecute.

The children were having fits during this evidence, and Tituba was asked if she could see who was afflicting them. She could. It was Sarah Good. Before long Tituba herself fell into convulsions. The women were examined again on March 3 and 5, and on March 7 were committed to Boston jail.

On March 11 a day of prayer and fasting was proclaimed in Salem. The girls threw fits, and one of them, twelve-year-old Ann Putnam, fingered Martha Corey, a reputable church member, as the one spectrally responsible. Asked what clothes the specter was wearing, Ann

Above: The Arrest of a Salem Witch, *by Howard Pyle. Business as usual. Authority: male, virile, stern; the opposition: female, frail, confused; the result: no contest.*

Opposite: *George Proctor on the scaffold*

There was now a pause in the examinations, but the spectral harassments continued. On March 19 the Reverend Deodat Lawson, formerly a minister in Salem Village, came to town. He spent his first night at Ingersol's tavern, and there saw Mary Walcott having a fit; on going to the Parris house nearby to pay his respects, Abigail Williams gave a hysterical show. The next day, Sunday, Lawson preached a sermon, "Christ's Fidelity the Only Shield Against Satan's Malignity," though not without interruption. One of the afflicted declared that his text was very long, and another saw a yellow bird perching on his hat as it hung on a nail by the pulpit. Undeterred, Lawson urged the magistrates to prove themselves "a terror of and punishment to evil-doers," though he warned there was no infallible way of discovering a witch: there was "no means instituted of God to make a trial of witches," he reminded the congregation, and cautioned them against false accusations and rash censure, which were themselves devilish behavior.

On the day of Lawson's return to Salem Village, a new accusation had been made, and this time against a woman of a very different background from those already jailed. Sarah Good was a destitute beggar, Sarah Osborn was old and sickly, and Tituba was a black slave. But now Rebecca Nurse, a God-fearing woman of property, a person of good standing in the community, was accused by the afflicted girls. Petitions by prominent people were drawn up on her behalf before the preliminary investigation on March 23 and before her trial; she modestly protested her innocence of the charges. She was convicted on June 30 and executed on July 19. On the day of Mrs. Nurse's examination, Dorcas Good, the daughter of Sarah Good, was also examined. All of four or five years old, she voluntarily confessed that she too was a witch, and had her own familiar—a little snake that used to suck her blood from a spot on her forefinger. Sure

replied she did not know, for she had been blinded. When men went to fetch Martha Corey to the magistrate, she asked if her accuser had told them what clothes she was wearing; before the magistrate she was asked how she knew the question had been raised. She was unable, or refused, to give a satisfactory answer, and, confirming her known skepticism about witchcraft, said "we must not believe all that these distracted children say."

During her examination Mrs. Corey sometimes bit her lip, and when she did the children complained of being bitten. This was, the Rev. Noyes of Salem Town explained, a form of image magic, in which Martha Corey used her own body instead of a doll to inflict harm. Off to jail with Mrs. Corey, to await further examination.

THE LAST MOMENTS OF GEORGE PROCTOR

When Elizabeth Proctor was accused of witch-craft, her husband George accompanied her to court, and for this was hanged; for in court, Abigail Williams and Ann Putnam, the hysterical girls who had accused his wife, accused him too. The accusation was considered to be proven when, on hearing it, their co-hysterics immediately fell into fits, and when Abigail, attempting to strike Proctor, found her fist made miraculously harmless. He was condemned forthwith. Later, on the scaffold, he was choked by the smoke from the executioner's pipe, and was unable to state his last words.

Below: The Trial of George Jacobs. *The elderly, and patently innocent Jacobs was accused of witchcraft by his grand-daughter Margaret. In time she came to her senses and retracted her accusation; by then Jacob's trial had begun, but the withdrawal of charges proved no impediment, and Jacobs was condemned.*

enough there was a small red mark there, about the size of a flea-bite. Who had given her the snake? Her mother.

Dorcas spent seven months in prison before the case against her was dismissed by the Superior Court of Judicature. In 1710 her father requested the General Court for compensation because "being chained in the dungeon [she] was so hardly used and terrified that she hath ever since been very chargable, having little or no reason to govern herself."

Having discounted social standing and acknowledged piety (in the case of Rebecca Nurse) and extreme youth (in the case of Dorcas Good) as grounds for rejecting the accusations of hysterical (and in some cases probably malicious) pubescents, the magistrates were now only two steps away from unleashing a torrent of accusations. First, they discovered grounds for believing that an organized conspiracy of witches was at work in Essex County, and secondly, they emphatically confirmed the validity of spectral evidence.

In the first matter, the afflicted girls made a good beginning. On March 31 a day of public fasting was declared on their behalf, and during the course of it Abigail Williams declared that the witches had decided to have "a Sacrament that day at a house in the village, and that they had Red Bread and Red Drink." The following day Mercy Lewis, Thomas Putnam's maid, said that "they did eat Red Bread like Mans Flesh, and would have had her eat some: but she had turned away her head and Spit at them, and said, 'I will not Eat, I will not drink, it is Blood.'"

On April 3 Sarah Cloyse, Rebecca Nurse's sister, caused a scandal by storming out of the Meeting House when the

Reverend Parris chose as the text for his sermon *"One of them is a Devil."* Like malignant weather vanes the afflicted girls caught the wind of scandal, and pointed at Sarah Cloyse as a communicant in the Devil's sacraments. She was examined the following day and jailed, but spent only some eight months in chains, having her case dismissed the following January by the Superior Court Judicature.

On May 10 Magistrate Hathorne took the second step towards unleashing a maelstrom of accusations. During his examination of George Jacobs Sr. he declared that although the Devil might choose to appear in someone's form, he could do so only with that person's consent. By decisively rejecting the strongest argument against spectral evidence, Hathorne turned resolutely from the course that would have voided all accusations made against the Salem defendants—the supposition that the girls were suffering from demonic possession, but that this was caused by the Devil and his impersonations alone, without the aid or agency of witchcraft.

Now the accusations came in droves. Whatever the original charge might have been, the accused was usually jailed on grounds provided by the afflicted girls during the preliminary examination. Among those arrested and subsequently hanged was a former minister of Salem Village, George Burroughs, who was brought from his parish in Maine for the privilege, and who not only gave a speech from the scaffold that touched his audience deeply, but recited the Lord's Prayer without error, a thing supposed impossible for a witch. By the end of the summer of 1692, nineteen people had been hanged on Witch's Hill in Salem Village. One man, Giles Corey, had refused to answer his indictment—had refused to plead either guilty or not guilty, or to agree that the court had a right to try him. He was therefore, as the law allowed, tortured by having weights piled upon his body until he either answered the indictment or died. Corey chose to die, and took two

Left: *Rev. George Burroughs on the scaffold. He had abnormal strength, and could, reputedly, lift a heavy fowling piece by sticking a finger into its barrel. This sign of a supernatural ability—one of the few non-spectral pieces of evidence presented at Salem—told strongly against him.*

Below: *Giles Corey: because he refused to plead guilty or not guilty as charged, the penalty of 'extreme and lengthy pain' was imposed. He was pressed to death by heavy weights, and after two days died in agony, but still silent.*

Below: *Blustery weather atop Salem's Witch's Hill; the condemned man takes a few last breaths of sweet air, and raises his eyes for the last time to the scudding clouds. And when this wonderful singularity, the living man, has been turned to a clod of meat on a rope, the clouds will still fly by, and his unmindful executioners will turn placidly to their next appointment.*

days about it. Under the weights his tongue was forced out of his mouth, but, as he lay dying, a kindly sheriff poked it back in again with his cane.

The most searing of the Salem trials was probably that of Rebecca Nurse, perhaps the most obviously innocent of those who died. The jury also thought her innocent, and returned a verdict of not guilty. When they did, Rebecca's accusers fell into a howling frenzy. Chief Justice Stoughton reminded the jurors of a piece of evidence they might not have taken into full account: an accused woman called Hobbes had been brought into the court to give evidence against Rebecca, who had protested because Hobbes was "one of us," meaning a fellow prisoner, and therefore (as she thought) not in a position to testify. But the words might have been taken to mean that Rebecca and Hobbes belonged to the same coven. When Rebecca—old, tired, partially deaf, afraid and exhausted after a day in court—was asked to

explain what she had meant, she made no answer. Her silence weighed heavily with the jury, and a new verdict of guilty was returned.

Rebecca's subsequent written explanation was that "I being something hard of hearing, and full of grief, none informing me how the court took up my words, and therefore had not opportunity to declare what I intended when I said they were of our company." Governor Phips granted her a reprieve. The afflicted ones immediately began a howling hullabaloo, and claimed renewed spectral attacks by Mrs. Nurse. A representation on their behalf was made to the governor, who withdrew his reprieve. Rebecca was then, in her own presence and without a dissenting vote, excommunicated by her church, and on July 19 was hanged, facing the gallows with every dignity and sign of Christian virtue.

Of the thirty-eight persons recognized by the civil or ecclesiastical courts in Massachusetts as afflicted in 1692, three

were male and thirty-five female. Twenty-three were teenagers or even younger, three were in their 20s, two in their 30s, and three in their 40s; for seven persons, no age was recorded. Twenty-nine persons were single, seven were married, one was widowed, and one was of unrecorded marital status. The largest category of the afflicted (twenty-one persons, almost 68% of the afflicted for whom an age was recorded) was of single girls, teenaged or younger. The smallest category was of married men (one person, John Indian, being of unrecorded age).

Second Thoughts and Confessions

With their successes in court, fame came to the afflicted, and other communities, such as Andover and Gloucester, began to seek their visionary help. (Though not every community respected their insight: on the way to Gloucester they stopped at Ipswich, threw a revealing fit or two, and were firmly ignored.) But at this peak in their affairs, success itself became their enemy. As others learned the methods of the Salem hysterics (or were infected by them), accusations became more and more numerous and incredible, and were increasingly directed toward the ruling classes. Targets included clergy (the Rev. John Willard of Boston), politicians (the Secretary of Connecticut), judges and justice (Nathaniel Saltonstall and Dudley Bradstreet), merchants (Hezekiah Usher and Philip English), military men (Captain John Alden), and the wives of prominent men (Margaret Thatcher, widow of a Boston divine and mother-in-law of Judge Corwin). There were also—a very bad mistake—rumors against the wives of the governor and Increase Mather. Moreover, as the charges became increasingly absurd, it seemed more and more obvious that legal procedures were merely aggravating the problem.

One novel method was used successfully against the accusers. A Boston man, accused by persons in Andover, sent

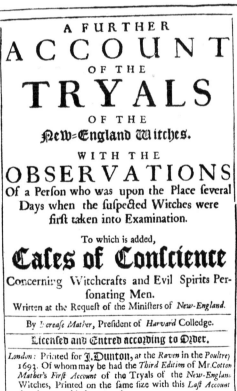

agents to the town to inquire, in a very public way, into those who were accusing him. In the course of their inquiries, these men let it be known that the accusers would soon find themselves facing a massive lawsuit for defamation of

Left: Increase Mather (1639-1723): a political as well as a religious leader in the Bay Colony, he was pastor of Boston's North Church from 1664 until his death, and in 1688 negotiated with England a charter for the merging of the Plymouth and Massachusetts Bay Colonies.

Below: A pamphlet containing an account of the Salem trials by Cotton Mather and Increase Mather's important Cases of Conscience Concerning Witchcrafts and Evil Spirits Personating Men. *In this the elder Mather criticized the use of "spectral evidence" in trials, and helped to bring prosecutions for witchcraft to an end in New England. The pamphlet was written and widely circulated in manuscript form in 1692, but was not published until the following year.*

Below: *The Judge's nightmare: an accused witch, beautiful and deadly, proves her occult powers as a lightning bolt bursts her manacles.*

character—£1000 in damages would be asked. This news had a rapid and wonderfully tranquilizing effect on the afflicted, who, upon making the shocking discovery that the law was a stick with two ends, quickly dropped their charges against the aggressive Bostonian.

An even worse blow was aimed at the afflicted by the theologians. After conferring with seven colleagues, Increase Mather, president of Harvard and the Bay's premier divine, drafted a pamphlet called *Cases of Conscience Concerning Evil Spirits Personating Men*. Publications on witchcraft in the colony had been banned as part of an effort to cool things down, but Mather's manuscript

circulated widely. He began by saying that no one, however virtuous, was immune to charges of witchcraft, and cited the Jesuit slander against Martin Luther as an example. He then stated a principle that no longer has much force with death-penalty enthusiasts, but which, in those unsophisticated days, carried some weight: "It were better that ten suspected witches should escape than that one innocent person be condemned." Most importantly, Mather put the full weight of his learning and moral authority against the use of spectral evidence to obtain convictions. With that compromised, the witchfinders lost most of their power, and the afflicted

began to be thought of as possessed rather than bewitched.

On October 12 Governor Phips ordered a moratorium on the trials, and on October 26 the Court of Oyer and Terminer ("Hear and Determine") was terminated. It had heard thirty-one cases, six of them against men, and had pronounced death sentences in every one. Of the eleven not yet executed, five were reprieved after making confessions, two died in jail, two had their executions postponed because they were pregnant, and were later reprieved, and one escaped. One, Tituba, was held until the court decided that it was unable to reach a decision about her, and was then sold as a slave to pay for the

costs of her imprisonment. Reprieves cost money, and those whose estates had not already been seized were sometimes bankrupted by the charges (as was William Buckley, who paid £10 for the release of his wife and daughter) or else remained in jail until someone paid their bills (as happened in the case of Margaret Jacobs, on whose testimony George Jacobs Sr. was executed, the court ignoring Margaret's retraction).

Confessions of Error

The Massachusetts trials are rare in the history of witchcraft in that most of those responsible for them eventually admitted their errors. On January 14, 1697, the Lieutenant-Governor, Assembly and Council declared a day of public fasting, because they believed that God was quite clearly still displeased with the Colony—He was "...diminishing our substance, cutting short our harvest, blasting our most promising undertakings... and by his more immediate hand snatching away many out of our embraces by sudden and violent deaths..." On the day of the fast, the twelve jurors in the trials signed an admission of error:

"We confess that we...were for want of knowledge in ourselves and better information from others, prevailed with to take up with such evidence against the accused, as on further consideration, and better information, we justly fear was insufficient for the touching the lives of any, Deut. 17.6, whereby we fear we have been instrumental with others, though ignorantly and unwittingly, to bring upon our selves, and this People of the Lord, the guilt of innocent blood...

We do therefore hereby signifie to all in general (and to the surviving sufferers in especial) our deep sense of, and sorrow for our errors, in acting on such evidence to the condemning of any person.

And do hereby declare that we justly fear that we were sadly deluded and mistaken, for which we are much disquieted and distressed in our minds; and do therefore humbly beg forgiveness....

BEFORE AND AFTER SALEM

From 1648 until the beginning of the Salem trials in 1692, legal action was taken in the Bay Colony against thirty-four people accused of witchcraft. Four of these (and probably a fifth—the records are imperfect) were executed. Most commonly, those found guilty of witchcraft were whipped, fined, bound over to keep the peace, or, occasionally, pilloried or put to the ducking-stool.

During the five months between the first legal actions at Salem (on April 21) and the last execution (on September 22), legal proceedings were instituted against 141 people. Of those, nineteen were hanged, and one, Giles Corey, was pressed to death for refusing to testify.

Thus, although the number of proceedings increased greatly during the period of the Salem trials, the ratio of those tried to those executed did not greatly change. For the Salem period the figure is approximately 7 : 1 (141 : 20), while for the forty-four preceding years the comparable ratio is 6.8 : 1 (34 : 5). In the rate of executions, however, the difference is extraordinary: in the years before Salem, there was one execution for witchcraft every 8.8 years, or 0.0095 executions per month; at Salem the rate was four a month—or 421 times as many. Yet within two years of the last execution, witchcraft ceased to be an actionable offense in the Bay Colony.

We do heartily ask forgiveness of you all, whom we have justly offended, and do declare according to our present minds, we would none of us do such things again on such grounds for the whole world, praying you to accept this in satisfaction for our offence; and that you would bless the inheritance of the Lord, that He may be entreated for the land."

Judge Samuel Sewall joined the jurors in their confession, in a statement given to the minister of the old South Church in Boston, and the minister read from the pulpit there while Sewall stood to acknowledge his guilt:

"Samuel Sewall...being sensible that as to the guilt contracted on the opening of the late commission of Oyer and Terminer at Salem (to which the order of this day relates) he is upon many accounts, more concerned than any he knows of, Desires to take the Blame and Shame of it, asking pardon of men, and especially desiring prayers that God, who has unlimited authority, would pardon that sin and all his other sins, personal and relative."

In 1706 Ann Putnam, who had been one of the principal accusers, and who by then was a young woman of 26, made her own confession. It was read in Salem Village church by Rev. Joseph Green:

"I desire to be humbled before God for that sad and humbling providence that befell my father's family in the year about 1692; that I then being in my childhood, should by such a providence of God, be made an instrument for the accusing of several persons of a grievous crime, whereby their lives were taken away from them, whom now I have just grounds and good reasons to believe they were innocent persons...but what I did was ignorantly, being deluded of satan. And particularly as I was a chief instrument of accusing of goodwife Nurse and her two sisters, I desire to lie in the dust, and to be humbled for it, in that I was a cause, with others, of so sad a calamity to them and their families; for which cause I desire to lie in the dust, and earnestly beg forgiveness of God, and from all those unto whom I have given just cause of sorrow and offence, whose relations were taken away or accused."

Left and below: *Judge Sewall, and a 19th-century version of his confession of error in the Salem trials.*

Opposite: *Common punishments for witchcraft in New England: the pillory and the ducking-stool.*

Overleaf: *Accusers arrive at a Salem home to make an arrest.*

Page 97: *Witch's Hill: site of the Salem executions.*

HARSH WORDS FOR THE ACCUSERS AND AN ESCAPE

The following account, unmitigated by credulity, of Salem's legal procedures and the way in which spectral evidence was obtained, was written by Captain Nathaniel Cary and printed in the Boston merchant Robert Calef's blast against the trials, *More Wonders of the Invisible World*:

"I having heard some days, that my Wife was accused of Witchcraft, being much disturbed at it, by advice, we went to Salem-Village, to see if the afflicted did know her; we arrived there, 24 May, it happened to be a day appointed for Examination; accordingly soon after our arrival, Mr. Hathorn and Mr. Curwin, etc., went to the Meeting-house, which was the place appointed for that Work, the Minister began with Prayer, and having taken care to get a convenient place, I observed, that the afflicted were two Girls of about Ten Years old, and about two or three other, of about eighteen, one of the Girls talked most, and could discern more than the rest. The Prisoners were called in one by one, and as they came in were cried out of, and so forth. The Prisoner was placed about 7 or 8 foot from the Justices and the Accusers between the Justices and them; the Prisoner was ordered to stand right before the Justices, with an Officer appointed to hold each hand, least they should therewith afflict them. And the Prisoners Eyes must be constantly on the Justices; for if they look'd on the afflicted, they would either fall into their Fits, or cry out of being hurt by them; after Examination of the Prisoners, who it was afflicted these Girls, etc., they were put upon saying the Lords Prayer, as a tryal of their guilt; after the afflicted seem'd to be out of their Fits, they would look steadfastly on some one person. And frequently not speak; and then the Justices said they were struck dumb, and after a little time would speak again; then the Justices said to the Accusers, 'which of you will go and touch the Prisoner at the Bar?' then the most couragious would adventure, but before they had made three steps would ordinarily fall down as in a Fit; the Justices ordered that they should be taken up and carried to the Prisoner, that she might touch them; and as soon as they were touched by the accused, the Justices would say, they are well, before I could discern any alteration; by which I observed that the Justices understood the manner of it. Thus far I was only as a Spectator, my Wife also was there part of the time, but no notice taken of her by the afflicted, except once or twice they came to her and asked her name....

Being brought before the Justices, her chief accusers were two Girls; my Wife declared to the Justices, that she never had any knowledge of them before that day; she was forced to stand with her Arms stretched out. I did request that I might hold one of her hands, but it was denied me; then she desired me to wipe the Tears from her Eyes, and the Sweat from her Face, which I did; then she desired she might lean her self on me, saying she should faint....

Justice Hathorn replied, she had strength enough to torment those persons, and she should have strength enough to stand. I speaking something against their cruel proceedings, they commanded me to be silent, or else I should be turned out of the Room. The Indian before mentioned, was also brought in, to be one of her Accusers: being come in, he now (when before the Justices) fell down and tumbled about like a Hog, but said nothing. The Justices asked the Girls, who afflicted the Indian? they answered she (meaning my Wife) and now lay upon him; the Justices ordered her to touch him, in order to his cure, but her head must be turned another way, least instead of curing, she should make him worse, by her looking on him, her hand being guided to take hold of his; but the Indian took hold on her hand, and pulled her down on the Floor, in a barbarous manner; then his hand was taken off, and her hand put on his, and the cure was quickly wrought. I being extreamly troubled at their Inhumane dealings, uttered a hasty Speech (That God would take vengeance on them, and desired that God would deliver us out of the hands of unmerciful men.) Then her Mittimus was writ. I did with difficulty and charge obtain the liberty of

a Room, but no Beds in it; if there had, could have taken but little rest that Night. She was committed to Boston Prison; but I obtained a Habeas Corpus to remove her to Cambridge Prison, which is in our County of Middlesex. Having been there one Night, next Morning the Jaylor put Irons on her legs (having received such a command) the weight of them was about eight pounds; these Irons and her other Afflictions, soon brought her into Convulsion Fits, so that I thought she would have died that Night. I sent to intreat that the Irons might be taken off, but all intreaties were in vain, if it would have saved her Life, so that in this condition she must continue. The Tryals at Salem coming on, I went thither, to see how things were there managed; and finding that

the Spectre-Evidence was there received, together with Idle, if not malicious Stories, against Peoples Lives, I did easily perceive which way the rest would go; for the same Evidence that served for one, would serve for all the rest. I acquainted her with her danger; and that if she were carried to Salem to be tried, I feared she would never return. I did my utmost that she might have her Tryal in our own County, I with several others Petitioning the Judge for it, and were put in hopes of it; but I soon saw so much, that I understood thereby it was not intended, which put me upon consulting the means of her escape; which thro the goodness of God was effected, and she got to Road Island, but soon found her self not safe when there, by reason of the pursuit after her; from thence she sent to New-York, along with some others that had escaped their cruel hands; where we found his Excellency Benjamin Fletcher, Esq; Governour, who was very courteous to us."

Myth and Magic

A myth is, of course, not a fairy story. It is the presentation of facts belonging to one category in the idioms appropriate to another. To explode a myth is accordingly not to deny the facts but to reallocate them.
—GILBERT RYLE THE CONCEPT OF MIND (1949)

Wherever the practices of witchcraft, sorcery and shamanism are found, the broad purposes of magic are the same: to explain, empower, and manipulate the social order. To these ends, its characteristic modes are those of transformation and divination.

Transformative magic can be broadly classed according to the sphere in which it operates: the natural world and elements, the human body and emotions, and the body politic. Sorcery dealing with the elements—earth, water, air, fire and space—ranges widely from alchemical and weather magic to the purificatory rituals of fire. (The European witch-burnings, for example, were partly purifying events: being a repository of evil, the witch's body had to be totally destroyed.) The casting of love spells, and spells seeking to create jealousy, anger, and dissension, work on the emotions. Other kinds of body magic seek to transform health, strength, and generative capabilities. Transformations within the body politic can seek an increase in personal wealth and power, an improved status for certain cliques, or an improvement in the standing and options of the society as a whole.

These forms of transformative magic are often combined, and are frequently used in conjunction with oracular magic, whose simpler goals are to seek information about the past, present and future: what has happened (was someone murdered, and, if so, by whom?). what is happening (is my husband or wife being unfaithful?), and what will happen (will I have a long, happy life?).

In most, but not all cases, both kinds of magic employ spiritual intermediaries of benevolent, malign, or neutral character. These beings, like the specific methods of magic, vary greatly from culture to culture, and stories of their exploits often form the framework of a tribe's history, or even explain the topography of the region it inhabits. If such beings, which may sometimes take the form of an animal ally or counterpart, are not directly involved in the magical work, some charm or spell empowered by them is used. Very rarely, a sage or sorceror attains such spiritual power that he or she can perform magic directly; but however diversely magic works, it serves preoccupations, and promotes experiences, that are recognizably consistent wherever they occur.

Opposite and below: *Masked dancers take part in a New Year festival at a Buddhist monastery in Qinghai Province, China. In Buddhism, techniques of transformation play a major role, and all phenomena are regarded as fluid, without a fixed character, always undergoing change. Here the five skulls surmounting the dancer's skull mask (opposite) signify the five Buddha families, and thence the transformation of what Buddhists call the Five Poisons: Ignorance, Aggression, Pride, Desire, and Jealousy. When transformed, these poisons become (in sequence) the Wisdom of the Expanse of Qualities, Mirror-like Wisdom, the Wisdom of Equality, Discriminating Wisdom, and All-accomplishing Wisdom.*

Opposite, above:
A young African boy submits to an ordeal test by a witch-cleansing cult: where the causes of illness and misfortune are seen as supernatural, witchfinders are still common.

Opposite, below:
A New Zealand Maori totem. Totemic systems ascribe spiritual partners to a tribe or social group; totem poles reveal the storied hierarchy of these invisible allies.

Below: *An African healing and purifying ritual using domestic chickens.*

BODY MAGIC
The Sky-Children of Cameroon

In the Mamfe division of south-west Cameroon the Bangwa people articulate a sophisticated system of witchcraft and animal alliances to help explain illness and to compensate for poverty and other social problems. Children are as likely as adults to be witches, and are called Children of the Sky. One of these, a twelve-year-old boy named Asung, became famous in Mamfe in the 1960s.

The rumors about Asung began when he fell ill. Shortly before that there had been a quarrel in the family compound between two of his father's wives, and a three-month-old baby had died. Asung was the son of one of the quarreling women, and when he developed what Western medicine would have diagnosed as tetanus poisoning—fever, delirium, severe muscular contractions—he was quickly suspected of being responsible for the baby's death, and before anything could be done to cure him, it was necessary for him to confess to this. He was questioned, and soon admitted that he had changed himself into a deer and had then "taken out" his snake to eat his half-brother. On its way back to the compound, the snake had cut itself on a broken bottle, and the muscular contractions had begun. Worse followed: Asung's were-elephant had been trapped in a swamp in the forest, giving the boy bad pains in his liver, the organ with which the elephant was cognate. Then his "rainbow" had drunk from a witch's bowl in the compound, and his large intestine had begun to swell, till he felt that his body would burst. Worst of all, Asung confessed that he had eaten another child that had recently died in the compound, and this child was now wrapped around his throat, so that he couldn't move his neck.

Asung had "gone to the sky" to help his mother in her quarrel. The principal chief and local leaders came to see the boy, to hear his story and decide whether, in the light of his murderous behavior, an attempt should be made to cure him. Officially it was decided that he should not be cured. Unofficially, and secretly, the boy's father arranged for him to be taken to the nearest hospital, which was thirty miles away in Bangwa. But before they reached the hospital, Asung died. A year later, in 1966, another child died, and Asung was held responsible for that death too.

If the child hysterics of Salem were often impelled by the heat of puberty, Bangwa's sky-children seem to be driven by hunger. Their excursions are often dreams of eating human meat, and are understood to take place not in the ordinary world but in a parallel dimension, and often through the agency of an animal companion or ally. A child can thus be eaten by a witch, but still survive. Cannibalism was practiced during the Bangwa's war with their Mbo neighbors, and so is not considered shocking. A fourteen-year-old boy, for example, admitted that he, his father, and other neighborhood witches had "been to the sky" to eat his small sister, who was then very ill. A goat was bought, and the boy described how he and his fellow witches had parceled out his sister's body

among them; the goat's meat was then divided among the witches in the same fashion and they were told to take it away and leave the little girl alone. She got better. One boy who had admitted to spectrally consuming a small child who had died, then had the child's body tied round his neck by its mother, who said: "Why should I bury valuable meat? Eat him. Eat him."

In order to be cured of an illness, a Bangwa witch must confess to witchcraft, and thus will often admit in shocking and vivid detail to supernatural misbehavior, usually stopping short of confessing to murder or another really serious crime. Often, a confession is rewarded with a meal of chicken, and sometimes a cure follows a confession rapidly, just as relief came to the afflicted Salem girls when the touch of the accused witch took back the demon that was plaguing them.

Were-Animals

The were-animals and sky-excursions of the Bangwa are examples, as are found in all magical systems, of power sought through transformation. In Europe the witch's doll was magically transformed from a simple image into something able to affect its real counterpart, and, like broomstick-riding, was the result of an empowering pact with the Devil, whose demons took the form of the witch's familiars. Despite their malevolent capabilities, the Bangwas' were-animals are not intrinsically demonic, and thus have a wider and richer range of associations than was permitted to the European witch's toads and cats. They are far more closely intimate, being associated not only with specific illnesses—whooping cough, for example, is conjunct with the leopard—but also with bodily organs. Thus a Bangwa autopsy can reveal, in the peculiarities of a person's internal organs, what were-animal a person has had. In some African witch-cleansing cults certain were-creatures (like the owl, whose forte is to hear well and to know what's going on) are used to help in the detec-

FAMILIARS IN A COLD CLIMATE

The last great shaman of the Netsilik Eskimos, who live along a broad coastal swath of the Canadian Arctic between King William Island in the west and Simpson Peninsula in the east, was called Iksivalitaq. Before he died, around 1940, he revealed the names of his seven protective spirits or familiars, his *tunraq*. The roster was:

Kingarjuaq: Name means "Big Mountain," though only an inch high and three inches long; usually lived in Iksivalitaq's mouth, but would sometimes run about on his hand. It was covered with red and black spots.

Kanayuq: "Sea Scorpion"; also lived in Iksivalitaq's mouth, where you could sometimes see its ugly head.

Kaiutinuaq: A dead man's ghost.

Kringarsarut: Another ghost, about the size of a needle. It had just one very small ear, and a crooked mouth.

Arlu: A very large, white killer whale.

Kunnararjuq: A black dog; no ears at all.

Iksivalitaq: The ghost of the shaman's grandfather.

A shaman's *tunraq*—his assorted ghosts, monsters, animals and even plants—were sometimes inherited from another shaman and sometimes came to him of their own accord. Occasionally they were willful. One unfortunate shaman, Anaidjuq, had a *tunraq* called *Orpingalik*, whose habit was to attack his master from the rear and make off with his testicles, which could be recovered only by Anaidjuq's falling into a trance and shouting vigorously. If a *tunraq* failed to accomplish some task ordered by its master or mistress (Netsilik shamans can be male or female), it turned into *kigdloretto*, a lunatic, angry, blood-thirsty "reversed spirit," which could usually be subdued only by the more powerful *tunraqs* of a shamanistic consortium.

Despite these difficulties, *tunraqs* were indispensable in quelling or raising storms and helping to find lost objects; they could even kill seals far out at sea and bring them to shore. A shaman could also use his *tunraq* to kill an opponent or even to help him fly through the air.

Above: *An Alaskan dancer: the psyche flourishes as well in barren landscapes as in tropical.*

tion of witches; in the Christian view, which holds transformation to be the province of Christ's vicarious atonement, such activity is called "using demons to cast out demons" and is forbidden.

The Indians of Chiapas State in southern Mexico take their intimacy with the were-animal to a further stage and see their animal counterparts, their *naguals*, as literally co-extensive with themselves, and as operating within a parallel world. In this comprehensive equivalence—at this level of integration between the person and his or her *nagual*—the possibility exists of communication between the seen and unseen worlds in which each operates: a kind of flickering back and forth between the human and *nagual* components that comprise the spiritual entity. In Chiapas the were-relationship is between a specific person and a specific animal and establishes no necessary connection between persons whose *naguals* are of the same species. Such relationships do obtain in totemic systems, which thus represent the fullest development of the animal alliance.

Just as magical alliances with animals are a worldwide phenomenon, so control over dangerous animals is a universal sign of spiritual prowess. In the New Testament Jesus is described as having this power ("Jesus was in the wilderness forty days and forty nights, and was with

Left: *Smoki snake-handlers of Prescott, Arizona. Snakes, which move without limbs, wings or fins, and seem, in shedding their skins, to suggest a kind of rebirth, are universally feared, revered, or both. Snake-handlers, whether Native American or Appalachian Christian, Old World or New, seek to demonstrate states of spiritual grace and power. Here, they are involved in rain-making.*

Below: *An African headache fetish.*

the wild beasts, and the angels ministered unto him" [Mark 1:3]). And the Muslim sage 'Ibn `Isa's (the fakir Shêik `Abû `Abd 'Allah Sîdî Muhammed ben `Isa as-Sofiani al Mukhtârî, born in AD 1465-6, also known as Shêikh al Kâmil, "The Perfect"), made the parallel claim that "the jinns…and the animals of the desert are devoted to me." Relics of 'Ibn `Isa include two panther skins (one preserved at Meknâs, the other at Ouzra near Palikao), on which he slept and prayed. He was able to charm wild animals, and render venomous snakes harmless.

Jesus is known to Muslims as `Isa bin Maryam, and members of the North African 'Isâwîyya ("Men of Jesus") cult are described as carrying snakes in their clothing and devouring basketfuls of live scorpions and poisonous snakes, as well as toads, lizards and "a jumble of loathsome and venomous creatures." Again, there is a Biblical parallel, in Mark 16:18: "They shall take up serpents, and if they drink of any deadly thing it shall not hurt them"—a key text for North America's contemporary Appalachian snake-han-

Right: *African Fox King: the sorcerer's costume distinguishes him from ordinary men, disguises his ordinary self, and endows him with whatever extraordinary powers his costume signifies. When the imagined or sought-for transformation actually takes place, the perfected sage, whether Buddha, Christ or Prophet, appears as a man again.*

dlers. Other parallels can be made with stories of Dionysus and with Orpheus, a champion charmer of wild beasts.

Followers of the 'Isâwîyya cult have been found flourishing from the Upper Volta to Mecca, Medina, Egypt, Syria and Algiers. They seem to have some affinities with Tunisia's Panther Men, and their influence was discerned in Kenya's Kikuyu "leopard men," the Mau Mau terrorists or freedom-fighters who successfully opposed British rule.

Love Charms and Magical Compulsions

The most popular forms of magic are probably those by which love, or at least the sexual use of another's body, is obtained. Most commonly the method involves using something taken from the subject of the charm, or imposing upon the subject something associated with the charm-caster. This last course is said to be preferred by the Gypsy love-charmer, who finds success by slipping some fragment, exudation or unspeakable effluvium of his or her own body into the food or drink of the love object and ensuring that it is consumed. More conventional love potions contain herbs. In Welsh tradition, a secret ingredient is added to mead (fermented honey), or wine made from rhubarb, cowslips or elderberry. The potion was used with

uncomfortable success by a Glamorgan man who plied a village beauty with it, and thereafter had no peace from her: "It was pitiful to see her following him. She would run through pools, over hedges, up hill and down dale only to catch sight of him. At last he got tired of her and wished to undo the spell, but he could not. The girl died, worn out with mental anguish."

When herbs are used in charms their virtue is often borrowed from some spiritual being. Johnny-jump-ups (*Viola tricolor*) were called Love-in-idleness or Heart's-ease in England, and were thought to be potent for love charms because an arrow, shot over-ambitiously by Cupid at the lovely but chaste Moon goddess Diana, was scornfully deflected by her and, on falling to earth, struck the little viola, infusing it with amatory

Above: *Oberon, Titania, Puck, and dancing fairies, by William Blake. In* A Midsummer Night's Dream, *the King and Queen of the Fairies are at odds with each other, and so the natural world has gone awry. The elements no longer co-operate: there have been floods, the corn rots before it ripens, and the seasons are changed about. "And,"* Titania tells Oberon, *"this same progeny of evil comes from our debate, from our dissension." By interceding with such nature spirits, the sorcerer could affect the natural world.*

Right: *The Aztec rain god Tlaloc*

power. This is the plant whose juice Oberon, King of the Fairies, uses to make Queen Titania fall in love with the rustic Bottom, a bad match in the first place, whom Oberon, in a fast act of transformative magic, has rendered entirely unsuitable by giving him an ass's head. In *A Midsummer Night's Dream* (II.1:169-176) Oberon tells Puck, a.k.a. Robin Goodfellow, a known consort of witches, about the plant, and bids him fetch it:

> Yet marked I where the bolt of Cupid
>   fell:
> It fell upon a little western flower,
> Before milk-white, now purple with
>   love's wound,
> And maidens call it Love-in-idleness.
> Fetch me that flower; the herb I
>   showed thee once:
> The juice of it on sleeping eyelids laid
> Will make a man or woman madly
>   dote
> Upon the next live creature that it
>   sees.

If a man has actually obtained the love of a good woman, but finds himself, by reason of witchcraft (what else?) unable to perform the manly act, he can undo the dreadful ligature (the "tying up" of

his necessary conduits) by procuring a knife with which murder has been committed and then, however gingerly, sleeping with it between his legs. Upon waking, he firmly declares: "As this knife has proved capable of killing a man, even so may my own body prove capable of lying with my wife." This remedy is favored in Macedonia, where the women probably keep their opinion of the metaphor involved to themselves.

According to the Dobu Islanders of the west Pacific, love charms are not only handy but indispensable to the species' survival. They believe that men and women have no natural desire for each other, but only mate because men are always bewitching women, and women are always bewitching men.

For those inclined to try their hand at a love potion, the advice of the 16th-century French jurist André Tiraqeau was: "Let husband and wife abstain totally from charms, cups, and other magical philtres of the sort, which are supposedly able to secure love. By mutual affection, rather, and in other honorable ways, let them evoke, preserve, and increase their love."

ELEMENTAL MAGIC

Like various manifestations of the human-animal alliance, from witch's familiar to the socially instructive totem, the elements themselves, air, fire, earth and water, are also subject to magical operations. Indeed, they naturally and constantly demonstrate transformation: wind fans fire, heat stimulates growth, vegetation decays into humus, water evaporates into clouds; heat and cold, wet and dry, all yield to each other and combine, by the hour and season. Beyond that, each element exists in many forms and many states, from pure to gross, and with each level are associated beings of different degrees of influence over their elemental sphere. Thus, with appropriate help, a weather witch may produce rain to end a drought, or hail to destroy an enemy's crops.

How Milarepa Turned a Horse into a Scorpion and Filled a Valley with Hail

An example of weather magic is found in the account by the great Tibetan yogin Milarepa of his mis-spent youth, before he turned to Buddhism and attained enlightenment. When he was still a young man, his father died and his uncle and uncle's family stole a large part of his mother White Jewel's property. She was distraught, and told Milarepa that unless he avenged her by black magic she would kill herself in front of him.

Milarepa set out to find someone to teach him magic, meeting four young men on his journey. At length they arrived at the dwelling place of a teacher called Terrifying Conqueror. Milarepa's companions offered Terrifying Conqueror some small gifts and asked him to teach them, while Milarepa offered all his possessions, and his body, speech, and mind. After about a year the students had learned a few simple acts of magic— causing thunder, and so forth—and the teacher dismissed them. But Milarepa knew he hadn't learned enough to avenge his mother, so he pretended to leave with his friends but then returned, and explained why he needed to learn more

Above: *The Valkyrie, Odin's storm-riding female warriors.*

powerful magic. Terrifying Conqueror thought about it, and then said that though he'd been offered many treasures for his most secret teaching, no one had offered him his body, speech, and mind or proved his sincerity as Mila had done. He agreed to teach him the most powerful kinds of black magic.

First, he sent Mila to a friend of his, a teacher called Ocean of Virtues, to learn the secrets of causing death and unconsciousness. Ocean of Virtues advised Milarepa to build a secure hermitage for himself, in which no one could see any doors or other openings, and when this was done he taught him the methods. Mila went to his secure retreat to practice them. After seven days, the teacher came to the hermitage and said that the

Below: *A sea devil, or especially ill-favored mermaid. As ancient sailors understood, the sea is full of unspeakable and dangerous things.*

seven days of incantation should be enough, but Mila said the magic had to work at a considerable distance and asked for permission to continue with it to make sure. So he did, for another seven days, and on the fourteenth day the teacher came and told him to expect certain signs that night.

Sure enough, that night guardians appeared carrying thirty-five bleeding hearts and heads, which they piled up around a mandala.

There had been a wedding in Mila's uncle's family, with a feast for thirty-five relatives. The aunt and uncle were outside the house, discussing certain details, when they suddenly saw scorpions, spiders, snakes, and toads where the guests' horses had been. One scorpion, as big as a yak, seized a supporting pillar of the house in its claws and started pulling it down; at the same time all the horses in the stables started rearing and kicking, and they kicked down the other supports. The house collapsed, and everyone in it was killed. Only two of Milarepa's enemies, his uncle and aunt, were now still living, but he decided to wait before destroying them.

After the wedding atrocity, the villagers plotted to kill White Jewel, but she threatened them with her son's black magical powers and told Mila of the plot. Fearful of revenge, the villagers returned the stolen plot of land, but White Jewel had already sent word to Mila to avenge the plot.

Just as the wheat was beginning to ripen, Mila set out for his village, disguised as a monk. It was going to be one of the best harvests on record. In the morning he began his incantations. Huge black clouds gathered, converged and flung hail on the fields: the crop was utterly destroyed, and great ravines were carved in the valley.

And this, as Milarepa told his students, long after he had abandoned black magic and by devoting himself to the Buddhist path had attained enlightenment, was how he "accumulated black deeds out of vengeance against my enemies."

Water Babies & Sea Demons

The greatest variety of beings associated with the elements belongs, perhaps, to the watery kind, who inhabit every wet environment from ponds to oceans, and who range in temperament from kindly to vampiric and fatally seductive.

The Washo people, whose territory straddles central Nevada and California in the United States, regard a class of beings they call Water Babies as among the most powerful and benevolent of the numerous spirits that surround them. They are small—about two-and-a-half feet tall—can be male or female, and have a reddish complexion. They have big hands, and speak Washo. They have families and children, just like humans, and they sometimes leave their footprints at the water's edge; Cave Rock, on the east shore of Lake Tahoe, is an impor-

tant place for them, and a road of white sand runs along the lake-bed from Cave Rock to the lake's northwest shore. The Cave Rock may be a sort of water-baby metropolis, because hereabouts they've been seen wearing ribbons, high-heeled shoes, and other fancy stuff.

A Washo called Dick Bagley told a story of how he'd met the water-babies. He'd been at an all-night ceremony near Genoa, and, as will sometimes happen, had fallen into the fire and more or less burned off his trousers, though without burning his skin. Therefore he improvised a kind of skirt from his jacket and set out to walk home. When he got to Wally's Hot Springs, he decided to have a swim. He took off what was left of his clothes, saw a female water-baby, and immediately lost consciousness (such is the power of these beings).

The water-baby took him down into the lake, under the water, and before long they came to water-baby country. They got out of the lake there, and set off along a path to a settlement, where the houses were made of obsidian. They went to the

chief's house, but he wasn't at home. Instead, they found about twenty female water-babies there, and they all made a circle around Mr. Bagley and sang to him. When they'd finished it was about time for him to go back, so the one who'd brought him took him back to the edge of the lake (the lake in water-baby country), and told him to dive in, and he'd have no trouble finding his way back. So he did that, and then he woke up under some overhanging tules. He put on his ragged clothes and went home.

When a person hears a water-baby sing one of the special songs, he or she has very little choice but to become a shaman. That happened to Sam Dick when he was about eighteen years old. He was lying on the sand by a river after bathing and noticed he was "dreaming, in my imagination." A water-baby came out of the water, "yellow looking, with a small round face, long hair, and naked," and told him to sing a funny song. Sam didn't really see all this with his eyes, and the water baby didn't show him everything, so he didn't know whether

Above: *Beach magic: macumba by the sea, Rio de Janeiro. Macumba, like voodoo and santeria, combines traditional African elements with elements of Christianity. Here followers of the popular Brazilian religion decorate the sand with flowers and celebrate with music.*

Above: Rhine-maidens breasting the waters, *by Arthur Rackham. In Wagner's Ring they are nymphs who guard the treasure of the Nibelungen dwarfs. Their prototype is the unreformed Lorelei, who lives in the dangerous narrows between Koblenz and Bingen.*

Davy Jones is the ruler of all water demons. ("Davy" is derived from Div, the same word from which we get Devil, and "Jones" comes from Jonah, who made a sacrifice to storm devils.)

These water demons are a varied lot. They include Nauganaga, a Fijian demon with a peculiar grudge against celibates, and numerous Polynesian sea-demons derived from still-born children whose bodies have been thrown into the sea. A vampiric marine creature haunts the waters off Malacca, and the Mosquito Indians describe Wihwin as a horse-like demon who rises from the sea to devour sailors. In North America's Great Lakes there are also fierce man-eaters, including Nee-ba-aw-baigs who, with other spirits, lurked beneath the water to ambush Hiawatha. Russian streams and lakes are the abode of *rusalkas*, beautiful female waters sprites, apt to tickle swimmers to death and to cause storms. They influence the luck of fishermen, and with their male counterparts, the *vodyannies*, are especially active around Pentecost (Whit-Sunday), when sensible Russians avoid outdoor bathing. During *Rusalka* Week, appeasing alcohol and eggs are poured on the graves of drowned relatives. A Malay charm also uses eggs to quell storms:

> Eggs of the house lizard, eggs of the grass lizard,
> Make a trio with eggs of the tortoise.
> I plant this pole thus in the mid-stream,
> (That) wind and tempest may come to naught.
> Let the white (ones) turn into chalk,
> And the black (one) into charcoal.

Kachina

When America's Hopi people first came up from the south they lived around Wupatki, near Arizona's San Francisco Peaks. After a while they began seeing strange creatures wandering around near their villages, so they sent a young warrior to find out what was going on. He climbed the mountain, and when he got near the top he heard a voice calling him,

it was a boy or a girl, but when it was done the water-baby went off home to Cave Rock. Later Sam learned five more songs "from the air," but the water-baby taught him his first song, and after that he had no choice but to be a "doctor." Otherwise, he would have died within four years. Water-babies teach men and women the songs of a shaman, but the Lorelei, the water nymph of the river Rhine who guards a hoard of underwater gold, sings bewitchingly, like the oceanic mermaids and sirens, only to lure sailors to their death.

There are a great many demons, male, female, and bestial, for a sailor to avoid. The seabed is the Devil's Locker, and

Left: A magic moment: masked dancer and mortal woman. The ancient scenario of a disguised or concealed god (or goddess) forming a liaison with a human woman (or man) is a universal parable for the inter-penetrations of the seen and unseen worlds.

Below: Mask of the Yam Cult, an African version of veneration for Green Power, the most fundamental of all politics.

apparently from out of the ground. He found the entrance to a *kiva* and went down into it. He found two people down there: one looked like a human, but it wasn't; the other didn't look like a human and definitely wasn't.

The one that looked like a human, who lived in the depths of the mountain, introduced the other, who was quite ugly—not to say alarming—to human eyes, with shining teeth and a pointed nose, as Chaveyo, an Ogre Kachina. Since Chaveyo was obviously one of those strange beings who had been wandering around the villages, and because good manners and prudence seemed to demand it, the warrior offered him some prayer sticks.

Chaveyo was pleased and said that whenever the Hopi offered them prayer sticks they would make rain clouds. This was the beginning of a helpful alliance.

Eventually the Hopi moved to the Three Mesa region, where they still live. They are farmers, and when the winter solstice comes the kachinas leave their mountain home and go to spend the

Above: *Hopi Buffalo Dancer: like his Aztec colleague Tlaloc (page 106) he is devoted to growth, carries a lightning-stick, and wears a fringed garment with decorative shin-pads.*

planting and growing season with them; at the summer solstice, when the corn is well-grown, they return to the San Francisco Peaks.

In the first half of the year, the Hopi honor the kachina with dances. The men dress up as kachinas and wear masks to represent them (even female kachinas are portrayed by men). Chaveyo wears a black mask, with a green mark on the forehead (which signifies the track of a snipe), and

he has white moons on his cheeks. He has a snout with teeth. He wears a ruff made of wildcat skin, a velvet shirt, white trousers and a knife.

Other kachinas are comparatively exotic. Ahöla, or Mong Kachina, or Chief Kachina, also called the Germ God (as in germination), has a mask made from a sieve-basket of woven yucca, covered with cloth and painted one-third green, one-third black and one-third yellow, with black stars on the yellow and green parts. He has an upturned beak, wears a fox-skin ruff, a white shirt, white kilt with sash and a woman's belt, and green moccasins. He usually carries a wand and a gourd full of ceremonial water and appears in the Solstice and Bean Dance Ceremonies.

Hé-é-é wears a black face mask with a beard, the hair hanging loose on one side, and on the other done up in a "maiden whorl" like a woman's. He wears a woman's dress with a wedding sash, red moccasins, and has another dress as a shawl. He carries a rattle, a bow, arrows and a quiver. There are two stories about Hé-é-é. At Second Mesa, they say he is the spirit of a young warrior, who, while "changing clothes" with his bride in a corn field, saw enemies sneaking up on his village. In a state of dishabille, but wearing trousers underneath his dress, he ran to the village, roused the people, and defeated the enemy. At Oraibi they tell a different story: Hé-é-é is a girl, who was doing her hair when enemies attacked her village; she rallied the men, as girls sometimes have to do, and they despatched the enemy to flight.

Hundreds of kachinas, representing wonderfully complex intersections of spiritual, social, and economic realms, are similarly described by the Hopi and honored in their ceremonies.

THE BODY POLITIC
The Azande Poison Oracle

While magic offers control, oracles offer certainty. Before their traditional way of life was lost, the Azande people of southern Sudan made regular use of oracles. However, custom and status required that when questions of the greatest importance arose, only the poison oracle, the highest of all, be consulted. Among such questions were:

Why had a wife not conceived?
What witch was responsible for someone's death?
Who should execute that witch?
Was a certain site a suitable place for a homestead?

Matters of adultery, tactics in war, the marriage of a daughter, a pact of blood-brotherhood and accepting employment from a European were further issues demanding the oracle's advice.

To use the oracle one needed only simple equipment: chickens, and a quantity of *benge* poison, a red powder derived from a creeping plant. In use, the powder was mixed with water to form a paste with strychnine-like properties, and the liquid from this paste was then squeezed into the beak of a chicken; the question was posed in such a way that the fowl's death or survival provided a positive or negative answer. A second, decisive, test was then made on another chicken to confirm or invalidate the first test. This time the indications for a positive and negative answer were usually reversed: for instance, if death had been chosen to indicate a positive answer in the first test, survival indicated the same result in the second.

The poison oracle was only performed by men, who were obliged to observe certain taboos. Prior to consulting the oracle they were not allowed to eat fish, elephant meat or certain mucilaginous vegetables, nor to smoke marijuana or have sexual relations. Women (and, usually, unmarried men) were excluded from the procedure, and if a man was too poor to own the necessary chickens and poison the oracle was consulted on his behalf by a wealthier relative or by someone with official status. The oracle thus served as a means of social control from

which women were entirely excluded, and in whose operation those of low social status were obliged to rely on their superiors. The principal European investigator of the oracle, E.E. Evans-Pritchard, found that the best way to obtain information about it was to employ it in the management of his own household; he found the oracle "as satisfactory a way of running my home and affairs as any other I know of."

Above: *A Chinese fortune teller: omens (such as the earthquakes that preceded the death of Mao Dzedong) are still regarded with concern in China's high political circles.*

Below: *Uluru
(Ayers Rock),
molten by sunset; it
still recalls a flux in
pre-human history
to Australia's abo-
riginal people.*

Explaining the Unthinkable

Magic provides not only a means of political action but also a framework within
which history and pre-history, social
forms and even topography can be
explained. This is so with Australia's
aboriginal people, who expound their origins and the history of the landscapes
they inhabit in stories of the pre-human
epoch known as Dreamtime.

The great monolith known as Uluru,
or in English as Ayers Rock, which cov-
ers more than three square miles and
rises 1000 feet, sheer from the desert, is
the subject of one of these explanations.
Originally, the aborigines say, there was
no rock here, just a big waterhole. A tribe
called the Carpet Snake People lived on
the dark side of the waterhole, and
another, the Hare-Wallabies, on the
sunny side. They lived in peace. One day
each tribe received an invitation from
the Mulga Seed People, who lived a long
way away in the Petermann Range, to

come and help with some important rituals. The Hare-Wallabies were too busy,
and didn't bother with the invitation.
The Carpet Snakes set off, but on their
way they met up with the exceedingly
lovely Sleepy Lizard Women and canceled their travel plans. Meantime, the
Mulga Seeds waited, and waited.

Eventually, they got tired of waiting
and sent the bell-bird, Panpanpalana, to
see what was wrong. When he came
back he said the Hare-Wallabies were too
busy to come, and the Carpet-Snakes
were too busy being married to the
Sleepy Lizard Women, and they weren't
coming either. This was a considerable
insult, so the Mulga Seeds made a monster out of mud and sticks and sang evil
into him. They called him Kulpunya
and sent him to punish the Hare-
Wallabies. He killed most of them. Then
the Mulga Seeds sent the Poisonous
Snake People to punish the Carpet
Snakes. They fought near Mutitjilda

Spring, near the great waterhole, and Kulikitjeri, the leader of the Poisonous Snakes, wounded Ungata, the Carpet Snake leader.

When Ungata's mother saw that, she was furious. She spat a magical substance called *arakunita* onto her digging stick and transformed it into an invincible weapon. With a single blow she knocked off Kulikitjeri's nose, and then she killed him. The Poisonous Snake People began to retreat, but on their way they came to the Sleepy Lizard Camp and set fire to it. When the Carpet Snake People discovered that Ungata had died of his wounds, they all sang themselves to death.

Now the Earth herself protested the killing. She raised up the great rock called Uluru out of the waterhole, and it still records the battle. Wanambi Pool is Ungata's blood, and a seventy-foot boulder is Kulikitjeri's nose. You can still see Kulpunya there, striking his various attitudes of attack, and the dead Carpet Snakes are scattered all around, looking like cylindrical stones. The landscape shows the Poisonous Snake People too, as they looked when they were marching to battle, but now, to some eyes, they seem just like desert oak trees straggling across the desert.

If supernatural agencies can explain the sudden rising up of the great Uluru monolith from the Australian desert, they have also been used to explain social events of great magnitude. On June 26, 1284, someone walked into the town of Hamelin in Germany and somehow kidnapped 130 of the small town's children. They were never found.

Later, new, supernatural details of a magical pied piper were added to the story. Hamelin had been suffering a terrible plague of rats when this stranger came into town. He was strangely dressed, in many colors, and for a price offered to clear the town of its plague. The town agreed; the man stepped into the street, began to play his pipe, and soon rats appeared from everywhere. Slowly they followed him through the

streets to the river Weser; the piper waded into the river, the rats followed him, and drowned.

When the piper had done his job, he asked for his money, but the town refused to pay him. On June 26, he returned to Hamelin, this time dressed as a hunter, wearing a strange red hat, and with a terrifying expression. Again he took out his pipe and played, and now children came into the streets and followed him, as if bewitched, to a mountain west of the town, and disappeared with him into a cave.

Above: *The Pied Piper of Hamelin: a European version of the magician as an exorciser-of-pests, animal as well as demonic, and a reminder that magical bargains, once struck, had better be kept.*

THE LOADED BONE

Australia's inland aboriginal tribes use an effective form of ritual execution known as "bone-pointing." The bone itself is a needle-like implement, usually from six to nine inches long and made from human or animal bone, or wood. Through the "eye" a string of braided hair is passed, and secured there with a vegetable gum. This device, called a *kundela*, must be charged with a killing spell before it can be used.

Sometimes, the spell alone is enough to kill its victim, and sometimes the spell and bone are used in conjunction with an image of the victim, either a model, in which some of the condemned person's hair or nail parings have been incorporated, or a drawing made on a rock wall. If a model is used, it is burned or left to rot, and as it burns or decays, so the victim's life comes to an end. If a drawing is used, the shaman repeats the victim's name as he makes the image, and then "sings" some animal ally to destroy him. Or, the sorcerer may stab the image from the collar bone to the heart, or symbolically remove its kidney fat.

In stubborn cases, or when the condemned person has run away, tribal executioners called *kurdaitcha* must be sent after him. Traditionally they wear slippers woven of human hair and cockatoo feathers, and, after covering themselves with blood, apply kangaroo hair to their bodies. A mask of emu feathers completes the costume.

The *kurdaitcha* usually hunt in pairs or in a threesome. They are professionally relentless, and, if need be, will track their quarry for years, always carrying the charm-loaded bone with them. When they finally corner their man, they approach within some 15 feet of him, and one of them points the *kundela* at him like a gun, and shoots the charm out of it,

When the spell strikes, the victim is said to tremble and froth at the mouth; his limbs become contorted, and he falls to the ground; he writhes in pain, but, often, his constricted throat emits no cry.

After a time these first symptoms pass. But thereafter the condemned person sickens and begins to waste away. Unless a powerful sorcerer can supply him with an antidote to the curse, his death, often attended by great pain, is certain, its cause invisible to autopsy.

While all this was happening the townspeople were paralyzed, unable to act. When they came to themselves they searched the mountain, but they could never find any trace of the missing children. The only clue—perhaps—came years later from far to the east of Hamelin. Robert Browning describes it at the end of his poem "The Pied Piper of Hamelin":

And I must not omit to say
That in Transylvania there's a tribe
Of alien people who ascribe
The outlandish ways and dress
On which their neighbors lay such stress,
To their fathers and mothers having risen
Out of some subterraneous prison
Into which they were trepanned
Long time ago in a mighty band
Out of Hamelin town in Brunswick land,
But how or why, they don't understand.

Magicians all over the world exorcise pests of various kinds (the *Thesaurus Exorcisorum*, published in 1626, which contains the Roman Catholic ritual for exorcism, also contains rituals for getting rid of caterpillars and locusts), and in 1553 a woman was burned as a witch for sending bags of fleas to infest Leipzig. Non-magical reasons for Hamelin's trauma have also been proposed. Perhaps the townspeople were remembering the German Children's Crusade of 1212, when a boy named Nicholas of Cologne led 20,000 children on a quixotic march to capture the Holy Land; they got as far as Italy, and most of them never came home. Maybe Hamelin's children were among these lost children. Or perhaps what really happened at Hamelin may be explained by a less dramatic event: a thirteenth-century recruiting drive made in lower Saxony by Bishop Bruno of Olmütz to find families to colonize his diocese in Bohemia. Records show many of the same family names in Hamelin and Olmütz, and perhaps the town did suffer a migration of its citizens to the east. The story is more reasonable, and far less satisfying, than Hamelin's tale of a demonic piper.

In similar fashion, magical interpretations of all local folklore may be viewed differently, through rational (scientific, historical, political or other non-magical) perspectives by outsiders to the culture. Some societies, whether economically

advanced or relatively "primitive," retain strong non-rational beliefs as central to their culture. In Hong Kong, for example, the design and orientation of new skyscrapers, into which are invested huge sums of corporate money, is never undertaken without the close involvement of a *Feng Shui* expert, who consults on the most effective ways to avoid offending local spirits and assure a beneficial plan of natural energies. A building with bad *Feng Shui* can result in all manner of disasters, from failure to prosper to the sickness and death of its inhabitants. Voodoo rituals and beliefs are crucial in Haiti's culture. In other societies, particularly European and North American, such rituals are often considered to be merely superstition. Yet all cultures, however apparently rational, are deeply embedded with magical, religious and superstitious tradition. In New York, London and Frankfurt, it is rare to find a building with a thirteenth floor, or to find a newspaper without horoscopes.

As the great French anthropologist Claude Lévi-Strauss wrote in his essay *The Sorcerer and his Magic*: "From any non-scientific perspective (and here we can exclude no society), pathological and normal thought processes are comple-mentary rather than opposed. In a universe which it strives to understand but whose dynamics it cannot fully control, normal thought continually seeks the meaning of things which refuse to reveal their significance. So-called pathological thought, on the other hand, overflows with emotional interpretations and overtones, in order to supplement an otherwise deficient reality."

In the real world, as in the world of magic, stranger is sometimes better.

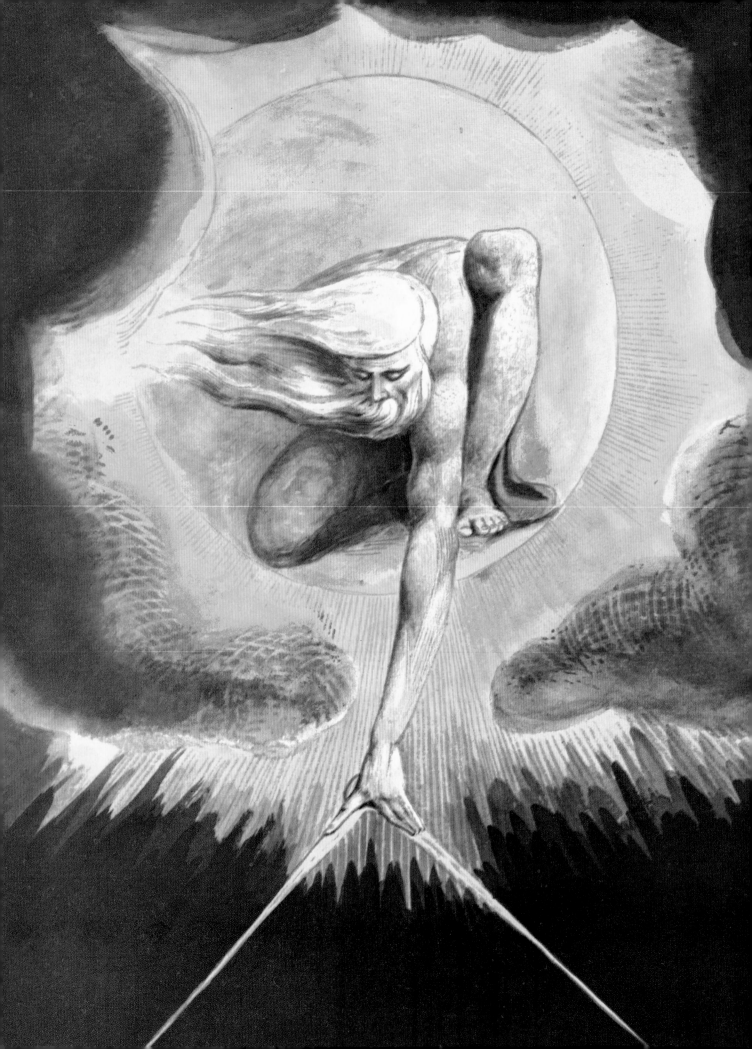

The Romantic Revival

The man who never alters his opinion is like standing water,
& breeds reptiles of the mind.

—WILLIAM BLAKE, *THE MARRIAGE OF HEAVEN AND HELL*

 By the early years of the 18th century the period of witchmania, no longer sustained by the social and political circumstances that once inspired it, exhausted by its own excess, and weakened by critical examination, was drawing to a close. The rationalist era had followed the philosophical revolution initiated by Descartes (1596-1650), and later developed by Hume and Locke. This world view no longer allowed God and the Devil to set the rules for the natural world; their new, more modest domain was strictly confined to the moral realm. Accordingly, the fire of the witch-finders was extinguished; witchcraft was perceived as merely illogical superstition, rather than the terrifying and potent Forces of Evil seen by the Church in the 14th to 16th centuries. Those who would once have been summarily burned at the stake were now tolerated, at worst dismissed as harmless or eccentric fools. Witchcraft, and society's preoccupation with the phenomenon, entered a dormant period until the later years of the 18th century.

But as the Age of Reason itself approached the cusp of a new century, heralds of a different mood began to be heard. In France Jean-Jacques Rousseau wrote that man "was born free, but he is everywhere in chains," and declared the natural nobility of the human condition was traduced on every side by social conventions. The American and French Revolutions of 1776 and 1789 effected massive overturnings of the established order, causing Thomas Paine

(in *The Rights of Man*, 1792) to reflect in wonder that "There was a time when kings disposed of their crowns by will upon their death-beds, and consigned the people, like beasts of the field, to whatever successor they appointed. This is now so exploded as scarcely to be remembered, and so monstrous as hardly to be believed."

In private quarters the winds of change were blowing even more fiercely. In 1793 the English poet and painter William Blake published *The Marriage Of Heaven And Hell*, taking a broader and more dismissive view of authority than even Paine, and turning upside-down most conventional views of good and evil, freedom and authority. In one section of this strange work, which he called 'A Memorable Fancy,' he tells the following tale. An angel comes to him, and urges him to consider "the hot burning

Opposite: The Ancient of Days, *from William Blake's* Europe: A Prophecy. *Blake's vision of history (it was dictated to him by a fairy he found sitting on a tulip) is prefaced by his engraving of God disposing Creation with a pair of dividers: "Times on times he divided and measur'd / Space by space in his ninefold darkness, / Unseen, unknown…"*

As the Romantic revolution progressed, God's role in society would be increasingly challenged.

Left: The radical political philosopher Thomas Paine, in a painting by James Watson. English-born Paine, who settled in America and strongly supported the American and French revolutions, was one of the period's most cogent opponents of authoritarianism and repression.

Below: *An engraving from William Blake's* The Marriage of Heaven and Hell.

Opposite, left: *The discovery of hypnosis, pioneered by Franz Mesmer (1734-1814), opened the doors to new vistas of psychological and occult inquiry in the late 18th and 19th centuries. Here a mesmerized criminal admits his guilt.*

Opposite, right: *By the 1890s hypnosis had become an important psychiatric tool; here French doctors observe a colleague putting his patient into a trance.*

dungeon thou art preparing for thyself for all eternity." Unabashed by this admonition, Blake coolly invites the angel to show him his fate, but says he in turn will then show the angel what lies in store for *him*—and they will then consider "whether your lot or mine is most desirable."

The angel leads him through a stable, into a church, and down into the vault, through which they reach a cave. Then:

"...down the winding cavern we groped our tedious way, till a void boundless as the nether sky appear'd ...By degrees we beheld the infinite Abyss, fiery as the smoke of a burning city; beneath us at an immense distance, was the sun, black but shining; round it were fiery tracks on which revolv'd vast spiders, crawling after their prey, which flew, or rather swum, in the infinite deep, in the most terrific shapes of animals sprung from corruption; & the air was full of them, & seemed composed of them: these are devils and called Powers of the air. Now I asked my companion which was my eternal lot? he said: 'between the black & white spiders.'

But now ...we saw a cataract of blood mixed with fire, & not many stones' throw from us appear'd & sunk again the scaly fold of a monstrous serpent...and now we saw it was the head of Leviathan: his forehead was divided into streaks of green and purple like those on a tyger's forehead: soon we saw his mouth & red gills hang just above the raging foam, tingeing the black deeps with beams of blood, advancing toward us with all the fury of a spiritual existence."

After showing Blake this hellish vision of his future, the angel leaves him, whereupon Blake finds himself sitting on a river bank in the moonlight, listening to a harper, who sings "The man who never alters his opinion is like standing water, & breeds reptiles of the mind."

Blake returns to the surprised Angel, who asks how he escaped, and Blake explains: "All that we saw was owing to your metaphysics; for when you ran away, I found myself on a bank by moonlight." Now it is the Angel's turn to see his fate, and Blake seizes him in his arms and they fly together in a westerly direction, until they are "elevated above the earth's shadow," reaching the void between the last planets and the stars. This space is the Angel's lot, Blake tells him. They see a church, and on the altar, a Bible. Blake opens it; it becomes a pit, which he enters, dragging the angel behind him. They come to seven houses and entering one of them find it full of carnivorous monkeys and baboons, where "the stench terribly annoyed us both."

"So the Angel said: 'thy phantasy has imposed upon me, & thou oughtest to be ashamed.'

I answer'd: 'We impose on one another, & and it is but lost time to converse with you whose works are only analytics.'"

Tygers of Wrath

Blake's refusal to accept the Angel's authority, and his description of the Bible as the doorway to a pit where only stinking primates chewing on their own flesh were to be found, reflects an

THE MAGNETIC SOMNAMBULISTS

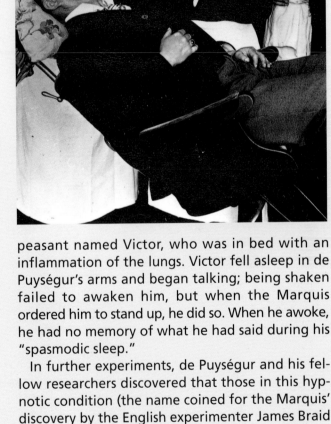

In the spring of 1784 the Marquis de Puységur, a French student of Franz Mesmer's theories of animal magnetism, magnetized a spreading tree on his estate at Busancy, near Soissons. Attaching long cords to it, he invited those needing relief from their ailments to come and test its healing powers. "Every leaf radiates health," he wrote, and many of those who came to sample the tree's power seem to have agreed. On one morning alone some 130 persons attached themselves to the tree by its cords and experienced the healing magnetic "crisis" (or *enfer à convulsions*—convulsive hell—as one observer described it) that was usually reserved for those able to afford treatment at one of the magnetic tubs or *baquets* then fashionable in Paris. (Patients sat around these tubs and obtained their magnetic benefits via movable iron rods that could be applied to any part of the body).

De Puységur had already cured his bailiff's daughter of toothache by magnetic means, and not long after magnetizing the tree he was treating a young peasant named Victor, who was in bed with an inflammation of the lungs. Victor fell asleep in de Puységur's arms and began talking; being shaken failed to awaken him, but when the Marquis ordered him to stand up, he did so. When he awoke, he had no memory of what he had said during his "spasmodic sleep."

In further experiments, de Puységur and his fellow researchers discovered that those in this hypnotic condition (the name coined for the Marquis' discovery by the English experimenter James Braid in 1843) could often diagnose their own illnesses, prescribe treatments, become capable of prophecy, and actually see the "magnetic fluid" as an aura streaming from the fingertips of the hypnotist and from other living beings. This "odic force" (the name coined by a German researcher, Baron von Reichenbach, in the account of his exhaustive experiments published in 1845), was also exuded by trees and minerals and could be passed through milk or water to produce a beneficial magnetic fluid.

Below: Storm in the Mountains *by Albert Bierstadt (1830-1902). A Romantic view of the brooding and awesome forces of nature*

Opposite, above:
The unsettling influence of the visionary realm: James Ensor's painting Demons Annoying Me *(1895).*

Opposite, below:
The Romantic celebration of intuition: the sorceress Morgan le Fay steals King Arthur's sword, in an illustration by Arthur Rackham.

extreme, but prophetic, anarchism. For the 19th century saw poets, artists and other seekers after spiritual truth place far more emphasis on the daemons of personal experience than on the virtues of established order. Their romantic impulse discovered new powers in the natural world, especially in those wild and craggy landscapes once shunned as contemptible. Those powers, rewarding, dangerous, and instructive, which had already appeared in a scientific guise in the findings of the French and German Magnetists (see previous page), appear in a purely romantic form in William Wordsworth's autobiographical poem *The Prelude*, in which he remembers his childhood as a pure, primitive state of the kind celebrated by Rousseau. After recalling scenes of running free in the radiant summer sunshine, surrounded by wildflowers and wooded hills, Wordsworth vividly describes how a childish prank precipitated a sudden transfor-

mation to a dark, frightening natural setting, and the onset of torment:

> *…for many days, my brain*
> *Worked with a dim and undetermined*
> * sense*
> *Of unknown modes of being; o'er my*
> * thoughts*
> *There hung a darkness, call it solitude*
> *Or blank desertion. No familiar shapes*
> *Remained, no pleasant images of trees,*
> *Of sea or sky, no colours of green fields;*
> *But huge and mighty forms, that do*
> * not live*
> *Like living men, moved slowly through*
> * the mind*
> *By day, and were a trouble to my*
> * dreams."*

The awe and danger experienced by the young Wordsworth were perhaps what Blake referred to in one of his Proverbs of Hell: "The tygers of wrath are wiser than the horses of instruction."

HEROISM, NATURE, NOSTALGIA

The Romantic preoccupations that helped to inspire 19th-century occult experiments—nature, freedom, personal endeavor, and nostalgia for bygone times—-emerge as clearly in the paintings as in the literature of the period.

The French genius Eugène Delacroix (1798-1863) exalted the heroic element in themes from history, literature, mythology and religion. His *Greece Expiring on the Ruins of Missolonghi* (1827), for example, is a characteristic tribute to Lord Byron, the English Romantic poet who died alongside Greek freedom fighters. In the hands of the English painter J.M.W. Turner (1775-1851), landscapes, seascapes and cloudscapes dissolved into celebrations of color, as if the natural world were reduced in them to an intrinsic or spectral luminosity. For the Pre-Raphaelites, who in 1848 declared themselves to be followers of nature and truth, nostalgia for medieval simplicity and beauty (in high contrast with the grime of the Industrial Revolution), combined with a gusto for high realism and literary symbolism, were instantly recognizable hallmarks.

Below: *A portrait of the Fox sisters by Currier and Ives, made in about 1850, some two years after they precipitated a worldwide interest in spiritualism. From left to right: Margaretta, Catherine, and their married sister Leah (Mrs. Fish).*

Opposite, above: *The Fox home in Hydesville, New York, where the mysterious rappings and communications from the dead began.*

Opposite, below: *On view at the Fox cottage in 1938: the alleged trunk of Charles B. Roena, the peddler purportedly murdered at the Fox house.*

Though the romantic impulse stressed the immanence of the divine above its transcendence, the principal English-speaking spokespersons for the romantic view were those Americans known as the New England Transcendentalists. Of these, the most effective was perhaps the indefatigable essayist and public speaker Ralph Waldo Emerson, who in "The Over Soul" (1841) addressed the notion of an intrinsic unity expressed alike in the natural and human worlds. "We see the world piece by piece," he wrote, "as the sun, the moon, the animal, the tree; but the whole, of which these are the shining parts, is the soul." Because all phenomena were rooted in an "over soul," they were connected, and "…the heart, which abandons itself to the Supreme Mind, finds itself related to all its works, and will travel a royal road to particular knowledges and powers."

In his essay "Nature" (1844), Emerson expanded upon his concept of how the secrets of the natural world might be unlocked with keys that were not only provided by nature, but were its very fabric:

"The whole code of her laws may be written on the thumbnail, or the signet of a ring. The whirling bubble on the surface of a brook, admits us to the secret of the mechanics of the sky. Every shell on the beach is a key to it…and yet so poor is nature with all her craft, that, from the beginning to the end of the universe she has but one stuff,…to serve up all her dream-like variety. Compound it how she will, star, sand, fire, water, tree, man, it is still one stuff, and betrays the same properties."

Emerson's discussions of the "royal road" were the intellectual companions of those radiant perceptions which in Thoreau's essays depict a natural world illuminated by a divine immanence, which give the nature poems of Keats their ravished numinosity, which shine and dazzle through Shelley's philosophical poems, and to which Wordsworth had added his intimations of awe before "the fury of a spiritual existence." Similar themes were evident in much of the art of the period.

In the new intellectual, artistic and political atmosphere of Blake, Emerson, Wordsworth and their fellows in the romantic movement, a fascination with spirituality and the occult emerged, a phoenix from the long-dead ashes of the witch-craze paranoia. Thus, barely recognizable, witchcraft was re-born in new guises for the 19th century, setting the tone for the rest of the millennium.

In 1848 revolutions broke out in France, Germany, Austria, Hungary, Bohemia and Italy; Karl Marx published the *Communist Manifesto*, and there had already been interesting socialist experiments in the United States (see page 133). At the home of the Fox family in Hydesville, in the town of Arcadia, New York, the invisible world seemed to be making its own effort to open the doors of perception.

Necromancy in Arcadia

Mr. and Mrs. John D. Fox had three daughters, Catherine (Kate), aged twelve, Margaretta, aged 15, and Leah, married and living nearby, and a married son, David. They moved to Arcadia in December, 1847, and almost immediately were disturbed by strange nocturnal bangings and rappings. On March 31, 1848, the whole family went to bed early, and the noises became fierce. The two children seemed unafraid, though, and Kate discovered that if she snapped her fingers and called out "Here, Mr. Splitfoot, do as I do," she obtained the same number of raps in response. When she held up her fingers, a corresponding number of raps was given. "Only look, Mother," she said, "look, it can see as well as hear."

Since it was still early, about 9 p.m., Mrs. Fox decided to call in some of her neighbors so that they could witness these strange events. Twelve or fourteen people were present, and one of them, William Duesler, recorded what proved to be the first seance of modern spiritualism.

The session, conducted by Mrs. Fox, was held in the family's bedroom. Many of the neighbors were too nervous to enter the room, but the intrepid Mr. Duesler went in and sat down on the bed. Mrs. Fox asked if Mr. Duesler's questions would be answered, and three raps sounded; Mr. Duesler "felt the bedstead jar."

"I then asked if it was an injured spirit, and it rapped. I asked if it had come to injure anyone who was present, and it did not rap. I then reversed the question, and it rapped. I asked if I or my father had injured it (as we had formerly lived in the house, there was no noise….I then asked if Mr. ——— (naming a person who had formerly lived in the house) had injured it, and if so, manifest it by rapping, and it made three knocks louder than common, and at the same time the bedstead jarred more than it had done before. I then inquired if it was murdered for money, and the knocking was heard. I then requested it to rap when I mentioned the sum of money for which it was murdered….and when I came to five hundred the rapping was heard. All in the room said they heard it distinctly. I then asked if it was five hundred dollars, and the rapping was heard."

Mr. Duesler then asked the spirit to rap his age, and the age of those others present in the room, which was successfully done. He followed by asking the number of children and the number of deaths in various families, and again got correct replies. When the spirit was asked its own age, it rapped thirty-one times; further questions revealed that the spirit had been a man, a peddler, and had left behind five children. It gave its initials as "C.R."

Above: *An upper class seance; by the end of the 19th century, seances were popular among all classes and gave successful mediums much prestige and social mobility.*

Over the next two days hundreds of people visited the Fox home to witness the rapping, and on Sunday the raps indicated that a murdered man (Charles B. Roena) had been buried in the cellar. In April (when the ground was soft enough) the family dug up the cellar and claimed to have found human hair and bones there. According to Sir Arthur Conan Doyle, excavations in 1904 confirmed this claim, but no independent corroboration of the crime, or even of the existence of a peddler named Charles Roena, was ever obtained.

As news of the Hydesville goings-on spread, the Foxes were met with curiosity and hostility. Margaretta went to live with her sister Leah in Rochester, and Catherine to stay at a boarding house in the nearby town of Auburn. The rappings followed them. Leah and a number of other people in Rochester proved to have mediumistic powers, and so did several guests in Kate's boarding house, at least one of whom was able to convey the gift to a friend of hers. In Rochester a group of friends formed the first Spiritualist Circle, and in November Kate and Margaretta gave their first public demon-

stration at Rochester's Corinthian Hall. Three investigating committees subsequently failed to find evidence of fraud in their performance, and the girls' fame, or notoriety, spread, inducing such celebrities as the novelist J. Fenimore Cooper and William Cullen Bryant, poet and coowner-editor of the *New York Evening Post*, to take part in—and be convinced by—seances.

Soon spiritualist circles were being formed in other states, and enthusiasts were not much deterred when, in 1851, three professors from Buffalo University claimed to have discovered the fraud by which the rappings were produced: the girls had a knack of cracking their toes and knee joints. *The New York Herald* reported that Margaretta Fox had admitted (to Mrs. Norman Culver, a relative by marriage) that the professors were right, and that Kate had shown her how the raps were produced. But still the enthusiasm for seances spread, and the spiritualist community was soon served by its own newspapers, ranging from Boston's *New Era* to *Light from the Spirit World*, which shone forth from St. Louis, and the *Yorkshire Spiritual Telegraph*.

became a subject of such obsessive interest that Michael Faraday, the leading scientific investigator of electricity, published a letter in *The Times* (June 30, 1853) describing experiments that proved table-turning was produced not by any electrical or magnetic force but by the conscious or unconscious muscular actions of those involved. This did nothing to check the public's enthusiasm, and various magnetic and psycho-electrical theories of the phenomenon flourished.

To these, in 1853, an old explanation was added: the Devil was doing it. The first news of this was published in Leeds by the Reverend N.S. Godfrey, who revealed that he had put a decisive stop to a session of table-turning by placing a Bible on the offending furniture and demanding that if the Devil be responsible for its antics he knock twice. He did. Skeptics repeated the experiment

Left: A French illustration of the table-tapping craze, which provided new insights into the capabilities of a hitherto humble article of furniture.

Below: The Medium by Hyman Bloom. For believers, spiritualism was the key to exotic wonders and a source of great comfort about the after-death state.

By 1854 there were enough convinced spiritualists in the United States for 15,000 of them to sign a petition urging Congress to investigate their claims. Congress was uninterested, and took no action, but the spiritualists were not abashed.

As early as 1852 London had had the privilege of its first visit from an American medium, Mrs. W.R. Hayden, who demonstrated table-turning and alphabetical rapping to the upper classes for half-a-guinea a head. Her performances were poorly received by the press, and one skeptic, G.H. Lewes, told his readers (in the *Leader* for March 12, 1853), that Mrs. Hayden's spirits had answered his mental inquires by revealing that the lady was a fraud, and that the ghost of Hamlet's father had seventeen noses. Some participants, however, including doctors, professors, and members of the aristocracy, received correct answers to their questions and were convinced that Mrs. Hayden's powers were genuine.

In the meantime, continental Europe had become engrossed in table-turning. When the craze reached England it soon

Below: *A demonstration of the remarkable properties of the trance state: a hypnotized woman defies gravity and the ordinary weakness of the muscular-skeletal system.*

using *Gulliver's Travels* and *Hoyle on Whist* instead of the bible, and found them equally effective. Mr. Godfrey undertook further experiments and published his results in a second pamphlet, *Table-turning, the Devil's Modern Masterpiece*: this time, he said, he had communicated with the spirit of a dead human, a former parishioner who had been sent to the seance from hell. The unfortunate being admitted that he had never attended Sunday school, save to enjoy a tea-meeting, and that his greatest current regret was that he had not, while still in the flesh, paid more attention to Mr. Godfrey's counsel. "Can it be," Mr. Godfrey wondered, in a bout of millennial italics, "that this is the

beginning of Satan's last struggle, that on the *imposition of hands* the table is endued with power *from the Devil,* as the Lord's servants *on the imposition of hands,* were, *in the Apostle's days,* endued with power *from on high?*" He pondered his question in a third work (*The Theology of Table-turning, Spirit-rapping, &c.,* 1854) and concluded that it was indeed possible: table-tapping, along with various newfangled economic and social ideas, was one of the signs of the Antichrist that was foretold in the bible.

Laypersons were quick to pick up the cue. Mr. R.C. Morgan's *An Inquiry into*

Table Miracles sold several thousand copies and addressed two questions: were manifestations of Satanic power possible? And, if so, was it probable that they should appear in the 19th century? Indeed it was, and the prophet Nahum (2: 3-4) provided startling evidence :

"The chariots shall be with flaming torches in the day of his preparation, and the fir trees shall be terribly shaken. The chariots shall rage in the streets, they shall jostle one against another in the broad ways; they shall seem like torches, they shall run like lightnings."

What else could these chariots be, Mr. Morgan asked, but the railway trains now running about the country, belching smoke, their carriages jostling each other, and, moreover, traveling on rails resting on sleepers often made of fir?

In 1854 Dr. Charles Cowan pursued this edifying theme in his *Thoughts on Satanic Influence, or Modern Spiritualism Considered.* Like Faraday, he found electrical explanations of spiritualistic phenomena deficient; unlike Faraday, he observed that Satan, being quite capable of such tricks, should be considered their probable agent. A clergyman from Bath, Mr. Gilson, agreed, but sounded a sectarian warning: he had attended a seance, he disclosed in his *Table-talking: Disclosures of Satanic Wonders and Prophetic Signs,* and in it a confessed demon had been asked where the Devil's earthly headquarters were. In England? (slight movement of the table); in France? (a vigorous movement); in Spain? (similar reaction); in Rome? (the table went wild). Another clergyman, Mr. Dibdin, weighed in: the devils *he* communicated with had assured him that the Pope was the head of the Christian Church, had recommended prayer to the Virgin Mary, and had confirmed that Luther was a bad piece of work.

It was in this atmosphere of millennial foreboding and popular excitement that the century's most successful medium, Daniel Dunglass Home,

"HOME, SWEET HOME!"
THE FRIEND OF THE SPIRITS.

arrived in England from the United States, bringing comfort to believers, puzzlement to skeptics, and consternation to Satan's foes.

Although he was perhaps most famous for his levitations, Home's repertoire contained little that had not already been done by his American counterparts (bodily elongations and the handling of hot coals were probably his most unusual effects). But he differed from most of his colleagues in the congeniality of his manner, in never charging for his seances, and in the ease with which he moved in aristocratic circles. Consequently, many eminent people—in England they included the art critic Ruskin (who hoped that Home would help him to converse with the great Italian painters), a former Chancellor of the Exchequer (Lord Lyndhurst), the painter Landseer, the novelist Thackeray, and Edwin Arnold, whose *Light of Asia* enjoyed transcendental status—were persuaded that there was in spiritualism a mystery, and perhaps beyond it a key, whether demonic or not, to still greater mysteries.

And indeed, several such key-bearers were at hand to unlock such mysteries.

Himalayan Masters

Helena Petrovna Blavatsky was born in Russia in 1831 and in 1847 married a man twenty-four years her senior. The marriage was short-lived, and, according to various sources, she spent the next several years of her life in diverse ways: as a bareback rider in a circus, studying with spiritual adepts in the Himalayas, teaching the piano in London and Paris, acting as an assistant to D.D. Home, and managing an artificial flower factory in Tiflis. In 1873 she visited the United States, found a turmoil of interest in spiritualism, and soon embarked on the activities that would make her famous.

A key event in Madame Blavatsky's new career was her meeting, at a Vermont farm belonging to two famous mediums, the Eddy brothers, with Colonel Henry Steel Olcott, who would spend the rest of his life as her devoted associate. At first she helped him investigate claims of fraud against mediums, and with her help (as he described in his book *People from Other Places*) he was able to affirm that Katie King—the same obliging spirit associated with Florence Cook, but then helping out a medium named Eliza White—was undoubtedly genuine. Unfortunately, spiritualism had

Left: A skeptical view of the era's most successful medium, the American Daniel Dunglass Home, from the magazine Tomahawk, *May 9, 1868. Although Home never charged for his services, the generosity of his patrons, indicated here by the materialization of coins and other financial instruments, allowed him to lead a very comfortable life in the highest circles of society.*

Below: Madame Helena Petrovna Blavatsky, in 1889. As the founder of the Theosophical Society, and a prolific author, she was perhaps the most influential occultist of the 19th century.

Opposite: *The conventions of 19th-century spiritualism as a 20th-century survival: like Florence Cook before him, the medium Nino Pecoraro is bound hand and foot and placed in a closed cabinet prior to the appearance of spiritual manifestations. Sir Arthur Conan Doyle, author of the Sherlock Holmes stories, and a firm believer in spiritualistic phenomena, was fully convinced of Pecoraro's authenticity. The photograph was taken in 1931.*

Right: *Madame Blavatsky and her partner, and co-founder of the Theosophical Society, Colonel Henry Steel Olcott. His interest in Buddhism helped to broaden Theosophy's multicultural appeal, and, despite being sometimes sorely tested, his faith in his partner's genius was never shaken.*

begun to lose its appeal in the United States. Blavatsky started a spiritualist newspaper, but it failed, and her Miracle Club, a mediumistic society that she started with Olcott, was another disappointment. News of her doings, most of it obtained from her associates in the mystical Brotherhood of Luxor, was still reported (for a modest fee) in *The Banner of Light*, but the time for a career change was clearly coming.

In September 1875, she and Colonel Olcott attended a lecture by a Mr. Felt on the mystical properties of the Egyptian pyramids. An understanding of the pyramids' occult proportions, Felt explained, permitted one to invoke certain spirits. Colonel Olcott, ever agog, suggested they start a society to study such things. HPB, as her followers called her, agreed, and so the Theosophical Society was founded. Within two years Blavatsky had written and published the society's compendious two-volume bible, *Isis Unveiled*.

This extraordinary *potpourri* of hermetic lore was a popular success. Its subjects ranged from Cornelius Agrippa (the teacher of Johann Weir, the witch-finders' opponent) to the Egyptian mysteries, the Pythagoreans, Kabbala, Hinduism and Buddhism. In preaching reincarnation (and thus marking Theosophy's split with spiritualism), it introduced its readers to much curious lore, including little-known information on what it termed the Root Races. These, Blavatsky explained, were seven in number: first, were invisible beings of fire and mist, who lived near the North Pole; second, the barely visible inhabitants of northern Asia, who invented sex; third, gigantic ape-like creatures—telepathic but unreasonable—who lived on the Pacific continent of Lemuria; fourth, the inhabitants of the now-sunken continent of Atlantis, who were destroyed by their addiction to Black Magic; fifth, humans; sixth, the race that will evolve from humans and return to Lemuria; and seventh, our grandchildren-descendants, who will eventually evolve from the New Lemurians and quit this planet in favor of life on Mercury.

FLORENCE COOK, MEDIUM EXTRAORDINARE

One of the grails of spiritualism was the "full body materialization," in which the fully embodied spirit of a dead person appeared to the sitters at a seance, and even moved among them. The first medium to achieve this in England was a teenage girl named Florence Cook, whose partner in the spirit world was Katie King, known in this life as Annie Morgan, daughter of the buccaneer Henry Owen Morgan.

The usual way in which a materialization occurred was for the medium to be seated in a cabinet, often after being physically examined (though less thoroughly than witches were used to) to ensure that she was hiding no illegitimate devices. She was then bound to a chair or couch with bonds verified by the audience to be secure, and the door of the cabinet was closed. Shortly afterwards the materialization would appear. When it had returned to the spirit world, the cabinet door was opened, revealing the medium still bound, often unconscious, and, of course, wearing the same clothes she had last been seen in—which were always quite different from the diaphanous costumes favored in the spirit world. Occasionally the materialized spirit could be seen at the same time as the medium, but then the medium's face was always covered by a shawl, or some other drapery, to protect her from the spirit-hostile light; if the medium's face could be seen, the face of the spirit was comparably draped.

Mediums and their spirits varied considerably. Florence Cook and Katie King were cheerful and coquettish. Another team, Mary Rosina Showers and her spirit colleagues Florence Maple, Sally, Peter, and Lenore, were of a more sinister cast, Lenore's appearance being usually accompanied by a displeasing odor of decomposition.

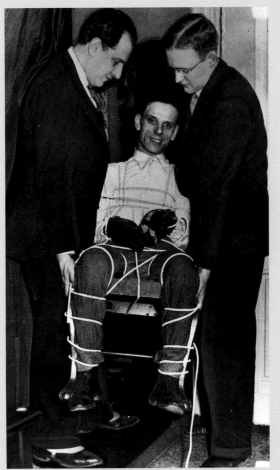

The following account of Katie King's last appearance, taken from *The Spiritualist* magazine for May 29, 1874, suggests why Florence Cook was the queen of English mediums in the 1870s:

"All the sitters in the circle clustered closely round her. Katie asked Mr. Tapp to take the bouquet to pieces, and lay the flowers out before her on the floor…She then divided the flowers into bunches for each, tying them up with blue ribbon.

Katie then took a pair of scissors and cut off a quantity of her hair, giving everybody present a liberal portion. She then took the arm of Mr. Crookes and walked all round the room, shaking hands with each. She again sat down and distributed some of her hair; and also cut off and presented several pieces of her robe and veil. After she had thus cut several great holes in her dress as she sat between Mr. Crookes and Mr. Tapp, she was asked if she could mend it, as she had done on other occasions; she then held up the dilapidated portion in good light, gave it one flap and it was instantly as perfect as at first.

She then appeared tired and said reluctantly that she must go, as the power was failing, and bade farewell in the most affectionate way; the sitters all wished her God speed, and thanked her for the wonderful manifestations she had given. Looking once more earnestly at her friends she let the curtain fall, and she was seen no more."

The "Mr. Crookes" referred to here was William Crookes, a distinguished psychical researcher who later became president of the Royal Society, and whose enthusiasm for pretty teenage mediums did not escape adverse comment.

By 1878 the Theosophical Society was established but in need of a boost, and HPB and Colonel Olcott decided it was opportune to visit India, where HPB had for some time been in occult communication with certain highly realized Mahatmas, including an adept named Koot Hoomi.

In Bombay Blavatsky and Olcott were a success. *The Theosophist* sold well, and the locals were impressed by Blavatsky's skill with the apport—the miraculously appearing object (a stock-in-trade of American and English mediums). She caused teacups and saucers to appear at picnics, made rose petals fall on the unsuspecting heads of pundits and scholars, and had a knack for finding lost objects. She also arranged for some of her favored disciples to communicate with her Mahatmas: replies to letters they gave her for delivery to these obscure beings appeared mysteriously in their rooms a few days later—seven volumes of them are preserved in the British Museum.

Colonel Olcott, meantime, set up more Theosophical centers in India, and in Ceylon, where he became a Buddhist and wrote *A Buddhist Catechism*. With the Society well established, Madame Blavatsky decided that she could afford to visit Europe, and accepted invitations

to Nice, Paris and London, where she agreed to let the Society for Psychical Research investigate her claims. While she was in London her housekeeper in India, a woman named Mme. Coulomb, *née* Emma Cutting, whom Blavatsky had taken in when she and M. Coulomb were down on their luck, sent evidence discrediting Madame Blavatsky and Koot Hoomi to *The Times* of London.

The redoubtable Blavatsky denied everything. She was now suffering from Bright's disease, but embarked on another book, a 1500-page marathon titled *The Secret Doctrine*: a work so cunning in its apparent disorganization, so resolute in following the labyrinths of wisdom, that only heavy bouts of editorial cutting and pasting made it at all comprehensible to ordinary readers. One who did read and comprehend was Annie Besant, the recovering ex-mistress of George Bernard Shaw. She entered Theosophy's fold, and when Madame Blavatsky died in 1891, three years after the publication of *The Secret Doctrine*, she was there to take up the reins, eventually publishing her own intricate classic, *The Ancient Wisdom*.

High Magic

In 1875, the same year that saw the foundation of the Theosophical Society in New York, Alphonse Louis Constant, better known by his pen name, Eliphas Levi, died in France. Twenty years earlier (coincidentally, the year of D.D. Home's first visit to London) he had published his first book, *Doctrine of Transcendental Magic*. In the intervening years he published several more books devoted to ceremonial magic: *The Ritual of Transcendental Magic* (1856), *The History of Magic* (1860) and, in 1864, a *Key to the Grand Mysteries*.

In the year of Levi's death a curious man named Eugène Vintras also died in France. While working as the manager of a cardboard box factory he had been visited by an old, raggedly dressed man, who had left behind a letter supporting the claims of one Karl William

THE CERESCO EXPERIMENT

For some forward-thinkers, spiritualism, magnetism and socialism formed a single, buoyant creed. One such was the American Warren Chase, a student of animal magnetism, who was also influenced by accounts of European theories of socialism.

Early in 1844 Chase and a few like-minded neighbors formed an association to establish a community based on principles described by the French socialist Fourier. They named the community Ceresco, after Ceres, the Roman goddess of fertility (the Greek Demeter), and began work.

The community flourished for six years, and Chase remembered it as follows:

"...a great stock and grain grower, raising in one season as high as ten thousand bushels of wheat. Had one genius [Chase himself] who did most of its preaching and law business, and others who attended to the sanitary department. Never used intoxicating drinks or allowed them on its farm. Never used profane language, nor allowed it, except for strangers.

Never had a law suit, nor legal counsel. Had little sickness, and no religious revivals. Never had a case of licentiousness, nor a complaint of immoral conduct. Lived a strictly moral, honest, upright, and virtuous life; and yet was hated, despised, abused, slandered, lied about, and misrepresented in all the country round about—mostly by preachers."

After the community disbanded, Chase spent the next thirty years of his life in politics, always moving toward the frontier (he eventually became a member of the California senate), and always true to his faith in his fellow men and in spiritualism.

Thus the life of this strange romantic, the World's Child, moved steadily from rationalism, by way of rewarding and revealing experiences of the natural world, to an unorthodox, but eventually influential, spirituality; and thus enjoyed a curious conformity with—even recapitulated—the historical processes by which occult optimism was revived in the late 18th and 19th centuries.

Below: *A Romantic devil, from* The Devil Walk *by Thomas Landseer (1831); the serpent that coils about this vigorous demon's leg carries the words "Evil Be" ("Honi soit")—the beginning of the motto of the noble Order of the Garter, "Honi soit qui mal y pense" ("Evil be to him who evil thinks"). Thomas Landseer (1795-1880) was the brother of Sir Henry Landseer, the famous Victorian animal painter.*

Opposite: *A sleeping girl in a hammock of roses is about to feel the arts of a modestly horned incubus; a 1913 illustration from the Russian magazine* Satyricon, *demonstrating some psychological distance from older views of the incubus and his victims.*

Naundorf, a German forger, to be the lost son of Louis XVI and Marie Antoinette, and therefore the rightful heir to the French throne. In a flash Vintras realized that the old man had been none other than the Archangel Michael and threw himself into Naundorf's cause. He built an altar in the factory, began to have visions, seemed able to cause consecrated wafers to bleed, and attracted many followers. He was arrested, with another agent of Naundorf's, and on slender grounds was sentenced to prison for five years. During his imprisonment a pamphlet was published that described his cult as devoted to obscenity and black magic. The charges were disproved by the police, and when Vintras was released from jail he declared himself to be a reincarnation of the prophet Elijah; he went to London, gathered more disciples, returned to France and there ordained a number of priests in his Church of Carmel. One of these was a defrocked priest named Joseph-Antoine Boullan, who, after Vintras' death, declared himself head of the Church of Carmel, and soon became embroiled in a magical battle with a disciple of Eliphas Levi.

This was the Marquis Stanislas de Guaita, who, with the help of a young Kabbalist named Oswald Wirth, had established a Rosicrucian order in Paris and who, in 1891, had published a vigorous attack on Vintras and Boullan titled *The Serpent of Genesis*: *The Temple of Satan.* Posing as would-be disciples, Guaita and Wirth had visited Boullan at his headquarters

in Lyons, and obtained secret teachings from him. They then disclosed that he and his disciples had long been addicted to black magic and the most repulsive kinds of sexual misconduct. Boullan, they said, taught that sexual intercourse was the way to salvation, and laid bare techniques by which his followers might enjoy dream-copulation with Christ, Mary, and the saints; he had fathered a child on a nun and had sacrificed it in a Satanic ritual; he had also published a magazine, with the witty title *Annals of Sanctity in the 19th Century*, that was devoted to Satanism. In short, Guaita said, Boullan was nothing but "a base idol of the mystical Sodom, a magician of the worst type, a wretched criminal," and informed him that he had been tried, *in absentia*, convicted and condemned.

To this, Boullan took grave exception. Assuming that his condemnation was magical, he sent forth a few spells of his own to counter whatever the Rosicrucians were up to, and for the next several years the French ether was busy with fusillades of spells and curses from both sides. One who caught a whiff of this magical grapeshot was J.K. Huysmans, whose novel of perverse romanticism *A Rebours* (*Against the Grain*) was a favorite with the hero of Oscar Wilde's *The Picture of Dorian Gray*. After consulting Boullan, who protested that he used only white magic to oppose the black Rosicrucians, Huysmans wrote *La Bas* (*Down There*), featuring a Black Mass and excerpts from the engaging life of the murderous pederast Gilles de Rais.

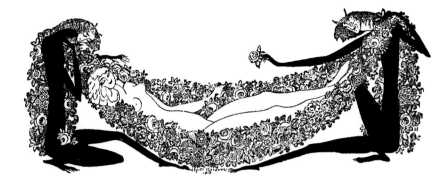

In 1893 Boullan died, and Huysmans and a friend named Blois accused the Rosicrucians of murder by magic. Guaita and Wirth denied the charges. Blois and Guaita set out to fight a duel, but en route Blois' horse came to a stubborn standstill, and at the dueling ground his pistol refused to fire, both events being taken as evidence of Guaita's magic. In 1897 Guaita, aged twenty-seven, died of a drug overdose, and the round of magical warrings came to an end. Across the English Channel, however, another round was about to begin. It would feature a translator of medieval grimoires, a poet turned theosophist, and a mountaineer, born in 1875, that year of high occult activity, who thought himself the reincarnation of Eliphas Levi.

A SITUATION OF THE MOST NOVEL PERIL

The following account of a "sitting" with the celebrated D.D. Home was written by Robert Bell, a dramatist and critic, and appeared in the *Cornhill Magazine* for August 1860. The magazine was then edited by the novelist William Thackeray, who vouched for the honesty of his correspondent.

"Mr. Home was seated next the window. Through the semi-darkness his head was dimly visibly against the curtains, and his hands might be seen in a dim white heap before him. Presently he said, in a quiet voice, 'My chair is moving—I am off the ground—don't notice me—talk of something else,' or words to that effect. It was very difficult to restrain the curiosity, not unmixed with a more serious feeling, which these words awakened; but we talked, incoherently enough, upon some indifferent topic. I was sitting nearly opposite Mr. Home, and I saw his hands disappear from the table and his head vanish into the deep shadow beyond. In a moment or two he spoke again. This time his voice was in the air above our heads. He had risen from his chair to a height of four or five feet from the ground. As he ascended higher he described his position, which at first was perpendicular, and afterwards became horizontal. He said he felt as if he had been turned in the gentlest manner, as a child is turned in the arms of a nurse. In a moment or two more he told us he was going to pass across the window, against the grey, silvery light of which he would be visible. We watched in profound stillness, and saw his figure pass from one side of the window to the other, feet foremost, lying horizontally in the air. He spoke to us as he passed, and told us that he would return the reverse way, and recross the window; which he did. His own tranquil confidence in the safety of a situation which seemed from below a situation of the most novel peril gave confidence to everybody else; but, with the strongest nerves, it was impossible not to be conscious of a certain sensation of fear or awe. He hovered round the circle for several minutes, and passed, this time perpendicularly, over our heads. I heard his voice behind me in the air, and felt something lightly brush my chair. It was his foot, which he gave me leave to touch. Turning to the spot where it was on top of the chair, I placed my hand gently upon it, when he uttered a cry of pain, and the foot was withdrawn quickly, with a palpable shudder. It was evidently not resting on the chair, but floating; and it sprang from the touch as a bird would. He now passed over to the farthest extremity of the room, and we judged by his voice of the altitude and distance he had attained. He had reached the ceiling, upon which he made a slight mark, and soon afterwards descended and resumed his place at the table. An incident which occurred during this aerial passage, and imparted a strange solemnity to it, was that the accordion, which we supposed to be on the ground under the window close to us, played a strain of wild pathos in the air from the most distant corner of the room."

Another witness of Home's levitation saw him float out through the window of an upstairs apartment and in again, feet first, through another.

Modern Times

Those who cannot remember the past are condemned to repeat it.
— GEORGE SANTAYANA *THE LIFE OF REASON* (1905)

 In the wandering cavalcade of 20th-century Kabbalists, Theosophists, Rosicrucians, Neo-Templars, Runic Magicians, Wiccans, Satanists, Dianists, postmodern pagans, Hasidic Druids for Jesus, and assorted other agents for the harmonious development and balanced polarity of humankind, one of the more colorful and repulsive figures is that of Aleister Crowley, alias the Great Beast, the only son of a wealthy English brewer.

The popular press called him the wickedest man alive, but since the competition for such an epithet was so fierce, this can hardly have been true. He believed himself to be a great poet, which was certainly not true, and the reincarnation of Eliphas Levi, which may have been, for like Levi he was a great inventor of magic for his times. His motto—Do What Thou Wilt Shall Be The Whole Law—still flutters the wings of contemporary Satanism, and his manners, now a valued part of political etiquette, consisted mainly in applying the boot to those weaker than himself. Crowley lent 20th-century magic many of those egotistical constrictions that other schools have since sought to replace with more open, humane, optimistic, useful, and—in short—female, methods. And it is between those two poles that the course of this century's magicians has generally shimmied.

The Superman: Cruel and Intrepid
Crowley's first, and last, teacher was MacGregor Mathers, born Samuel Liddell Mathers in London in 1854, and also known as the Comte de Glenstrae, the Chevalier MacGregor, and leader of the Hermetic Order of the Golden Dawn. This organization, for which Mathers devised rituals, translated grimoires and generally served, or ruled, as chief magus, probably had more influence than any other organization on the course of 20th-century magic. Its members included the poet W.B. Yeats, the Irish Nationalist Maud Gonne, A.E. Waite (who designed what is still the most widely used deck of Tarot cards), the writers Algernon Blackwood and Arthur Machen, Gerald Kelley, later President of the Royal Academy, and, in 1898, the twenty-three-year-old Crowley, an undergraduate at Oxford University.

Opposite: The Birth of the New Age *by Ms. B. Adams; from Bibby's Annual, 1911. An androgynous Good Shepherd, with orderly horned beasts and bearing a radiant Lamb, ushers in an era of promise.*

Below: *A sketch of Conan Doyle, creator of Sherlock Holmes, made in South Africa in 1900. Doyle was a tireless supporter of spiritualism.*

THE MAGICIAN   THE HIGH PRIESTESS   THE DEVIL .

Above: Cards from the Tarot deck designed by the American occultist A.E. Waite.

Right: Aleister Crowley, photographed during his 1934 libel suit against the author and publishers of Laughing Torso, *by his old friend Nina Hammett, in which he was described as a Black Magician. After hearing descriptions of Crowley's activities, the judge observed that "he had never heard such dreadful, horrible and blasphemous stuff," and the jury found for the defense.*

Even as a youth, Aleister inspired some fear and loathing. Though he applied himself to his books of magic, he was refused admission to an advanced grade in the Golden Dawn hierarchy because, as Yeats said, "we did not think that a mystical society was intended to be a reformatory." Annoyed but undeterred, Brother Perdurabo (the name he had taken in the Order, meaning "I shall endure"), took himself to Scotland, where he adopted the kilt and, forsaking the title he had adopted in London (Count Vladimir Svareff), appointed himself the Laird of Boleskine. On the shores of Loch Ness he applied himself to Kabbalistic magic, as described in Mathers' translation of *The Book of Abrahamelin the Mage.* Having already had partial success with this magic—materializing the head and left leg of a spirit called Buer—he succeeded in inducing a small army of specters to parade about Boleskine House and Lodge.

He was soon in need of them. Mathers, ousted from the Golden Dawn in 1900 for his autocratic ways, was living in Paris, and there he received another affront: a

letter from Crowley advising him that he, Crowley, had been appointed head of the order by its "Secret Chiefs."

Mathers had himself revealed the existence of these terrible beings. In a manifesto addressed to the members of the Second Order of the Golden Dawn in 1896, he had disclosed the following:

"As to the Secret Chiefs with whom I am in touch and from whom I have received the wisdom of the Second Order which I communicated to you, I can tell you nothing. I do not even know their Earthly names, and I have very seldom seen them in their physical bodies.... They used to meet me physically at a time and place fixed in advance. For my part I believe they are humans living on this earth, but possessed of terrible and superhuman powers....My physical encounters with them have shown me how difficult it is for a mortal, however 'advanced,' to support their presence.... I felt I was in contact with a force so terrible that I can only compare it to the shock one would receive from being near a flash of lightning during a great thunder storm, experiencing at the same time great difficulty in breathing....The nervous prostration I spoke of was accompanied by cold sweats and bleeding from the nose, mouth, and sometimes ears."

Crowley expected no reply to his letter, and received none. "I declared war on Mathers accordingly," he wrote, and war he got. The etheric channels between Paris and Loch Ness were abuzz with malice: first Crowley's pack of bloodhounds died, and then a beautiful female vampire was sent to destroy him. Fortunately, Crowley knew how to cope: he "smote the sorceress with her own current of evil," which perhaps means simply that he afflicted her with a heavier dose of perverse sex than she could handle. Whatever his method, his *Confessions* describe the poor vampire after their encounter: "The girl of twenty had gone; before him stood a hag of sixty, bent, decrepit, debauched. With dribbling curses she hobbled from the room." Despite this defeat, Mathers kept up the pressure, and Crowley's Lodgekeeper, no doubt a Presbyterian, and unused to magical attacks, lost his mind and tried to kill Crowley's wife Rose, who had been unstable to begin with, and had not been improved by life with the Great Beast, a name first given to little Aleister by his mother and fondly retained by him.

Below: *Rose Kelly, Crowley's unfortunate first wife. She married The Beast on a whim, was soon driven to drink, and, upon losing her mind, was promptly divorced by him.*

In response to these outrages, Crowley dispatched Beelzebub, and forty-nine demons of horrific appearance (Rose saw them), to Mr. and Mrs. Mathers' Paris apartment. MacGregor survived the attack, and lived until 1918, but the Order of the Golden Dawn did not, in either its London or Paris incarnations. Mather's wife Moina founded an offshoot, the Alpha Omega Lodge, when she returned to London after his death.

In 1907 Crowley founded his own magical group, the Order of the Silver Star, and in 1912 obtained the leadership of

KING OF THE MOUNTAIN

Among Crowley's exploits in Mexico, he climbed Mt. Popacatapetl, and attempted, by the sheer power of his concentration, to make his image disappear from the mirror into which he was gazing. In Cairo he dressed in oriental robes, called himself Prince Chioa Khan, and spent a night in the Great Pyramid of Cheops with his nervous wife Rose, the mother of his daughter, Nuit Ma Ahathoor Hecate Sappho Jezebel Lilith Crowley. He explored the Irrawaddy River in Burma (Myanmar) by canoe and studied yoga in Ceylon. In 1902 he failed in a serious attempt to climb K2, the world's second highest mountain, and in 1905 was chosen to lead an attempt on Mt. Kanchenjunga. On that expedition, he showed the quiet but firm resolve in the face of adversity that marks all would-be supermen.

The first serious setback emerged when the party reached Camp VII, at an altitude of 24,000 ft. (7,300m) There the Swiss climbers Guillarmod, Reymond and Pache called a meeting at which Crowley was sacked as the expedition's leader on the grounds of his abominably cruel treatment of the porters. Naturally he refused to accept this decision, and the expedition was canceled. While Crowley and Reymond stayed put at Camp VII, Guillarmod, Pache, and the Italian climber de Righi set off down the mountain. On the lower slopes—

as if the very gods of the high places were displeased—an avalanche buried the three renegades and the porters.

Guillarmod freed himself and de Righi, but Pache and the porters were deeply buried. Struggling to free them, Guillarmod and de Righi called out for help. Reymond raced down the mountain, but Crowley remained calmly in his tent, and that evening composed a letter, later printed in an English newspaper, in which he explained that he had had no inclination to help, because "a mountain accident of this kind is one of the things for which I have no sympathy whatever." In the morning he strolled past Guillarmod, de Righi and Reymond, who were still trying to recover the bodies of their companions, and made his way alone back to Darjeeling.

No further attempts were made to climb Kanchenjunga for the next twenty-five years, but Crowley continued to display icy nerve in the face of things for which he had no sympathy. Those included his mother (whom he called a "brainless bigot"), and his wife Rose, whom he divorced when she became insane. (In Ceylon she had once imagined that she was a bat, and had clung to the frame carrying the bed's mosquito-netting; thereafter Crowley, when the mood took him, suspended her upside down by her heels in a wardrobe).

Like many of the strong and wealthy, Crowley thought that no one should be protected from "the results of their own inferiority." Whether he took the same view of the much fouler consequences arising from suppositions of superiority is not recorded, but he probably did not.

the British section of a German group devoted to sexual magic, the Ordo Templi Orientis (Order of the Temple of the Orient, the OTO). He spent the period of World War I in the United States writing propaganda for the Germans. He later claimed that he had deliberately made what he wrote absurd, to subtly weaken the German cause, and that in New Hampshire he attained to the high magical grade of Magus by performing a ceremony in which he baptized a frog as Jesus Christ and crucified it. Neither story did much to endear him to his fellow countrymen.

In 1920 Crowley removed himself and his then mistress, Leah Hersig, also known as the Scarlet Woman, and the Ape of Thoth, to Cefalu in Sicily. There he named his home the Abbey of Thelema, covered its wall with obscene murals, and practiced sexual magic with his house guests. Meanwhile, the OTO was flourishing in various branches and styles, some of them in the United States. The organization had been founded in 1902 by an industrialist named Karl Kellner, who claimed to have learned his sex magic in India from Hindu tantrists. OTO also claimed to have discovered the sex secrets of the Knights Templars (whose leaders were executed as devil-worshipping heretics in the middle ages), and outlined a philosophy in which "all of Nature," not to mention freemasonry and alchemy, was interpreted in sexual terms. In 1914 OTO centers were established in Vancouver and Los Angeles by a disciple of Crowley's named Charles Stansfeld Jones, and the German OTO authorized a New York advertising man, Harvey Spencer Lewis, to open an American branch. However, Lewis was drawn to the Rosicrucians, and in 1915 founded the Ancient and Mystic Order Rosae Crucis in San Jose. In 1922 Crowley became head of the OTO; his appointment offended many, and the Order fragmented.

Meanwhile, in Germany, another group, the Order of the New Templars, also founded before the 1914-18 War,

proved more politically durable. Its guiding light was an Austrian anti-Semite, Adolf Lanz, who preached Aryan blood-purity, Germanic paganism, astrology and, strangely enough, Kabbala. The Germanen Order, founded in 1912, was also strongly anti-Semitic, and similarly devoted to sound Aryan—Teutonic/Nordic—practices, including rune-magic and the worship of the god Wotan. A third cult, the Invisible Aryans, practiced rune-magic too, but in an admirably straightforward way: they performed exercises in which they yodeled while twisting their bodies into the shapes of runes.

Above: *An assistant of Superman J. Weissenberg, self-styled Messiah and Prophet, lays hands on a believer. In 1929, Weissenberg's cult claimed 120,000 German followers.*

Opposite: *Aleister Crowley dressed as a Hierophant in the Order of the Golden Dawn.*

Right: A caricature of Rasputin, the cleric whose healing powers gave him authority over the Russian Tsar; he is portrayed with the symbolic elements of the occult Superman.

Below: Bishop Homer A. Tomlinson, claiming to be the rightful ruler of the world. The parallels with the Superman phenomenon of the occultists are clear.

The playwright August Strindberg was a member of the New Templars, and Adolf Hitler himself read and was influenced by Lanz's magazine, *Ostara*. The extent of Hitler's involvement in the occult is disputed; the Nazis employed an astrologer, a Swiss named Franz Krafft, but apparently only for propaganda purposes. They also believed that the British were locating their U-boats, deep below the Atlantic, with the help of pendulum-swinging dowsers, and to counteract this unsporting advantage the Berlin Pendulum Institute, founded in 1942, employed a variety of psychics. More interesting, in the context of 20th-century superman-magic and its Antichrist extensions, is a story told of Hitler by one Rauschning, the Governor of Danzig, and strongly reminiscent of MacGregor Mathers' words to the Second Order of the Golden Dawn. Hitler began by speaking of possible mutations of the

human race; Rauschning observed that all one could do was to work with nature. Then Hitler said: "The new man is living amongst us now! He is here! Isn't that enough for you? I will tell you a secret. I have seen the new man. He is intrepid and cruel. I was afraid of him." As he spoke, Rauschning says, "Hitler was trembling in a kind of ecstasy."

Not too long after Hitler had died in his bunker, one of America's own makers of supermen, or, at least, a salesman of blueprints for the job, took part in an experiment in Pasadena, California. The date was 1946, and the man was Lafayette Ron Hubbard, then a writer of science fiction, but soon to be the discoverer of

Dianetics and Scientology. He was working with Jack Parsons, who was head of the Crowleyite OTO Church of Thelema, and Parson's plan was to create an incarnation of Babalon, Crowley's name for the Mother Goddess. To do this, Parsons and Hubbard had to conjure up an elemental spirit to be the mother of the child, and this they did—she had green eyes and came from New York. Unfortunately, no child was conceived, perhaps because, as Hubbard would explain later, he had only taken part in the evil experiment to make sure that nothing came of it.

But Hubbard did go on to explain where supermen—he called them Thetans—came from and how we could discover our inner Thetan. He did this five years after his Pasadena adventure in a handy little volume called *The History of Man*. In it, he described the events by which we humans have come to be in our present sorry condition—the measure by which we fall short of our original superhuman status.

Originally, according to the book, we were all Thetans. We could do anything, including creating universes for our own amusement. But we got bored. So—about sixty trillion years ago—we curtailed our omnipotence to make life more interesting, deliberately abandoning our superhuman powers. But eventually we forgot that we were originally divine and had to endure a series of extremely uncomfortable circumstances for uncountable eons of time. We all carry around with us the unconscious memories, or engrams, of these unpleasant experiences. They rob us of our freedom—they prevent us from remembering that we are really Thetans. Hubbard's discoveries, and the techniques of Scientology, permit us to become conscious of our engrams and eliminate them. We then realize our true superhuman nature and become Operating Thetans once more.

The following are some of the classes of engrams identified by Hubbard. Stage One engrams derive from the millions of years we spent in the CLAM condition.

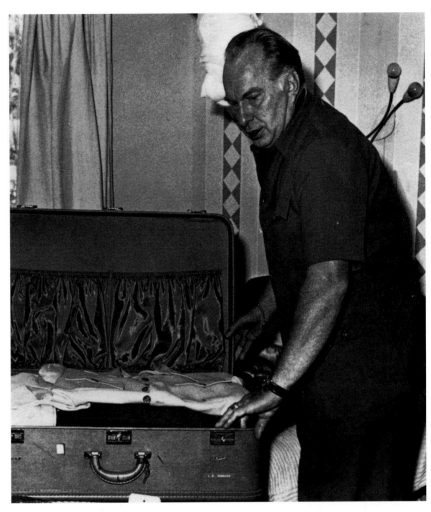

A good Scientology auditor can determine whether a person is suffering from CLAM engrams quite simply: he (or she) merely asks: "Can you imagine a clam sitting on a beach, opening its shell very rapidly?"—and simultaneously makes a rapid opening-and-closing movement with his or her finger and thumb. Upon this, one who is Clam-afflicted will "grip his jaws with his hand and feel quite upset"—and not because he fears he has fallen into the hands of a lunatic.

Another engram-generating phase, in which we've all spent more time than we care to remember, is THE PILTDOWN MAN, characterized (Hubbard tells us) by "freakish acts of strange logic…of eating one's wife and other somewhat illogical activities."

Examples of the engrams which afflict us include THE-JACK-IN-THE-BOX: examined too closely, it explodes, as it were, in the Thetan's mind, "filling his

Above: *Lafayette Ron Hubbard, discoverer of Dianetics, and founder of the Church of Scientology, packs his bags on leaving Rhodesia (now Zimbabwe).*

Below: *The Mount Carmel compound of David Koresh and his followers, near Waco, Texas, in flames after being attacked with tear gas by federal agents on April 19, 1993. Reports of the cult indicate Koresh's Superman complex, one aspect of fringe religious cults that alarms relatives of the converted.*

beingness full of pictures which are extremely confusing, being pictures of boxes of pictures." The alert auditor will recognise the presence of JACK-IN-THE-BOX engrams in those of his patients who are obsessed with cereal boxes—the ones that show pictures of cereal boxes that show pictures of cereal boxes...and so on.

Such are the hidden burdens we all bear. When we die, we report to a way-station in the afterlife for a "forgetter implant," usually on Mars, but it can be a sub-station: "The last Martian report station on earth was established in the Pyrenees."

While L. Ron Hubbard's *History of Man* can, arguably, make Madame Blavatsky's account of man's ancient origins (see page 130) seem the work of a sober academic, it was a bestseller, and it was, apparently, read as much for instruction as for amusement.

Not all modern Satanists believe in Satan literally, though some do. For many, Satan is merely a symbolic figure who serves as the fastest way of rejecting God and taking a pot shot at Christianity, which all good Satanists despise as a religion of the weak. Like Crowley (and Hitler) they revere the strong and the independent, finding those virtues in the story of Satan's refusal to serve. The method is therefore to glorify the self, and the tone of this practice is caught in a New Zealand magazine of the Left Hand Path, *The Watcher*; the following extract is from "Uncle Setnakt Says," an advice column in the April, 1992, issue (vol. vii):

"5. Encourage the worship of yourself by others...Certainly don't be a jealous god, you can help others in their self deification...When you've created a little friend and fan club, begin to practice the simple Lesser Black Magic of telling the story that people who do good things for you have good things happen to them (and the converse). Continue this practice at least until ...some good has come your way because someone you do not know (directly) has been told you're a worthy individual by someone else you do not know directly. This will show that your presence is equal in force to any of mankind's created gods—that faith in you is strong enough to create a missionary movement. Of course this should be done secretly and subtly. If you outwardly proclaim your godhood crucifixion can result. Christianity may be understood as one self-deified individual letting his practices get out of hand. Jesus is an example of a Black Magician without ethics."

In fact, Satanism constitutes a revival of the historical Judaeo-Christian tradition of witchcraft. Satanist beliefs are more recognizable to Christians than to the neo-pagans, most of whom completely reject Christianity, and with it, the Devil. Here is part of a Satanic view of the Apocalypse, contributed to *The Watcher* by Christos Beest, of the United

Left: Anton Szandor La Vey, of the First Church of Satan, in stern mood, dog-collar and full clerical garb; his wife, Diane, is in the posture of an acolyte.

Below: The Rev. Christopher Neil-Smith demonstrates his technique. One of the few clerics authorized by the Bishop of London to perform exorcisms, his services were in much demand in the early 1970s by parents of unruly—demon-possessed—teenagers.

Kingdom's Order of Nine Angles" (*sic*), "From the dark pool beneath the moon." The contempt for other occultists is expressed with a bile fully reminiscent of the magical battles of the late 19th and early 20th centuries:

"For those puffed-up comfortable occultists with their armchair ethics and pseudo-intellectual bullshit, it is all too easy to proclaim how the times are changing. Do these people actually understand what is meant by the 'New Aeon'? ...Waste your life if you will, poring over 'occult' books, absorbing correspondences, standing in basements and shouting out silly names! Fools! Occultists do not have the power and the understanding to grasp the events that will occur all too soon for their wretched lives. They still carry within them the sickness of the Nazarene. So good riddance to the scum and the pretenders!

Once it was necessary to remain silent, but now the cosmic tides are aligned and we shall be seen to finally shatter the tyrannical grip of Yeshua the deceiver."

Another Satanist, Anton Szandor La Vey, who formed the "First Church of Satan" in California in 1966, after his various careers (including lion-tamer and palm-reader) ran aground, borrowed heavily from the Christian tradition in his manifesto, *The Satanic Bible*. He advocated the pursuance of the seven deadly sins of Christianity as helpful in attaining control and power, and installed in his church and home altars, candles and other Christian paraphernalia.

Below: The Druidess by Rover Lionel. An early focus of neo-pagan interest, Druidism, the ancient religion of the Celts, enjoys a diverse popularity.

Superwomen

While Aleister Crowley was the world's most famous magician (he died an impoverished heroin addict in 1946), the second most famous magician in England was Violet Firth, better known by her pen name, Dion Fortune. She was also involved in a famous magical battle, which she made immortal in her classic work *Psychic Self-Defense* (1930).

In 1920 Ms. Firth, who had been raised by Christian Scientists, joined Moina Mathers' Alpha Omega Lodge, an offshoot of the Order of the Golden Dawn. She and Mrs. Mathers quarreled, and upon Ms. Firth's unsuspecting head a

plague of foul-smelling psychical tomcats was released; they were black, their morals were disgusting, and their leader was Moina Mathers in the form of a giant tabby. Ms. Firth struggled—on the astral plane—with this beastly emanation, and finally (thanks to Psychic Self Defense) subdued it. Thereafter she lived quietly close to Glastonbury Tor (the English seat of Arthurian Romance), wrote many books, including *The Mystical Qabalah* (1935), and died in the same year as Crowley.

In a sense, the course of witchcraft (or, more properly, Wicca, goddess worship and neo-paganism) in the second half of the century really is a story of psychic self-defense, by and for women. It owes much to two volumes by a woman, Margaret Murray's *The European Witch Cult* (1926) and *The God of the Witches* (1960). In these, Murray, a professional Egyptologist, proposed that the confessions of Sabbat attendance by accused witches, though obtained under torture, were largely true, and indicated the existence of an organized but secretive religion of witchcraft, whose focus was not the Christian Satan, but the ancient Horned God.

Although Murray's thesis has been repeatedly demolished by scholars, its vitality has proved that a peck of psychological relevance can easily outweigh a bushel of inaccuracy. However, it was not for more than forty years after her first book's publication that Murray began to find a widely sympathetic audience, and when she did it was largely because a man, Gerald Gardner, had found a way to make witchcraft appealing, and because, in 1951, England impetuously repealed the last of its anti-witchcraft laws.

Gerald Gardner was born in England in 1884 and spent most of his professional life in Ceylon and Malaya as a rubber and tea planter and a customs official. He returned to England in 1937 with an interest in knives, nudism, and the supernatural. In 1939 he joined a Rosicrucian group, the Fellowship of Crotona, whose

members included the daughter of Annie Besant, former head of the Theosophical Society. Through the Rosicrucians he met a witch coven, was initiated into the Craft by a woman known as Old Dorothy, and (he was also an initiate in the OTO) apparently paid Aleister Crowley to write some rituals for him. In 1949 he published a novel about witchcraft, *High Magic's Aid* (under the pen name Scire), followed in 1954 by his influential book *Witchcraft Today*, which revealed the existence of covens in England. Many interested people wrote to him, and with the help of the *Book of Shadows*, a recently composed 16th-century witches' handbook, and Gardner's own instructions—a ragbag, or perhaps a synthesis, of Crowleyism, folklore, Masonic symbolism, Eastern Religion, nudity, and as much flagellation (a hobby of Gardner's) as they could stand—formed covens of their own. With his guidance the movement spread into the United States, France and Germany. Once established, and in the absence of any central authority, covens tended to find their own way, pursuing

their own interests, and devising their own rituals. When a witchcraft museum was established on the Isle of Man, Gardner became its resident witch, and principal publicist. He died in 1964, resolutely non-Satanic, leaving witchcraft in a fluid but vigorous condition, and much preoccupied by the question of how authentic the Gardnerian and other claimed transmissions really were. His legacy was particularly apparent in the activities of Alex Sanders, who turned away from his earlier Devil-worshipping to lead covens in ritual magic and nude sabbatic gatherings.

In time, several schools of witchcraft were established in Europe, North America, Australia and New Zealand. By the late 1960s several patterns of practice had emerged, which were classified by Isaac Bonewits in his book *Real Magic* (1971) as neo-pagan or Wicca, neo-classical, neo-gothic, Classical, Family

Left: *Horned, feathered and masked, and with sword of enviable length, Alex Sanders is caught here in an informal moment in 1985. Author of witchcraft's Alexandrian tradition, he was declared King of Witches.*

Below: *Britain's best-known witch of the 1960s was Sybil Leek, shown here with her "medium," a jackdaw named Jackson. She answered hundreds of letters a week which sought her (and Jackson's) advice.*

Above: Erda the Earth Goddess, *by Arthur Rackham. A concern for ecological issues is a mark of much contemporary witchcraft (especially in those branches with a feminist bent) and helps to distinguish the craft from Satanism.*

Traditions, Immigrant Traditions, and a miscellaneous sixth group in which he included voodoo and Amerindian magic. Of these groups, Bonewits later (1976) estimated that neo-classical witchcraft had the greatest following, amounting to some 70% of practitioners in North America; he also divided the estimated 10% of neo-pagans into 5% feminist and 5% neo-pagans.

In this scheme, a Classical witch is primarily interested in those arts that were once primarily female and rural: herbal-

ism (including the preparation of medicines, poisons and hallucinogenic brews), midwifery, divination and the casting of spells. The context of these undertakings is without a particular religious bias, so the neo-classical witch may be sectarian, atheist or agnostic. Neo-gothic witchcraft, on the other hand, reflects the image of witchcraft that emerged during the years of persecution, and appears as a kind of mirror image of Christianity, so Satanism can be considered a subset of neo-gothic witchcraft; Bonewits estimates that between 2% and 3% of North American witches belong to a broadly neo-gothic class. Neo-pagan witchcraft follows the lines primarily suggested by Margaret Murray and expanded in part by Gardner and such contemporary feminist witches as Z. Budapest. Here, a variety of older traditions, such as Greek, Roman, Kabbalistic, Nordic and Celtic (including the older Druidical sects) is freely drawn on to produce new syntheses. Family and Immigrant traditions, each accounting for 1-2% of the witchcraft community, are, as their names suggest, derived from information passed down within a fairly narrow family or cultural context, and are likely to represent a direct transmission of knowledge and practice. The early preoccupation with the authenticity of, for example, the Gardnerian transmission, involved a discussion of whether Old Dorothy was really the representative of an ancient tradition of the kind Margaret Murray had described.

Today, concerns about authenticity are less pressing than they once were, and none of the divisions described above are watertight.

Traditions, youthful or not, are fluid, and are freely borrowed in whole or part, and as spiritual, social or political preoccupations change (for example, the ecological content of much contemporary practice is relatively recent) so does the focus and style of witchcraft's rituals. Some are rather intellectual and involve complex visualizations—"pathworkings"—whose scenarios seek to lead the practitioner through a hierarchy of spiritual levels, often with a Kabbalistic bent. Other rituals are simpler, more emotional, and make more use of dance and physical gestures. Traditions from the annals of witchcraft also survive, virtually stripped of their witchy connotations, in practices such as horoscope reading and water divining (sometimes called water-witching).

In general, those for whom witchcraft works don't care very greatly about its historical roots, while those who do care, often passionately, are increasingly to be found in the millennarian neo-witchfinding cults of the fundamentalist Christian far right, whose adherents have their own axes to grind and fires to light.

Yesterday, Today and Tomorrow: New Witchfinding

For many, all forms of witchcraft and neo-paganism are offensive and immoral. Some Christians maintain that witchcraft, like all occult practice, is the work of Satan, by whom its followers are deceived. They look upon the feminist witches as godless destroyers of family values, diminishing the man's role as the spiritual head of his family, and therefore deeply threatening society. Wiccans, neo-pagans, overt Satanists, and even atheists with no occult connections, are seen by some as heralds of the last days, of the coming Apocalypse, as front-runners of the Antichrist.

While such extreme views are the province of a minority of Christians, those who subscribe to them do so fiercely, bolstering their beliefs by a kind of quasi-Talmudic bibliolatry. Like the magician who sees the world as a text where all secrets are hidden, these fundamentalists expertly rake the Bible, and especially the Book of Revelation, for signs of the last days, for clues to that desirable time and place when they and the rest of the saved will be "raptured" into the sky, safe above the End Times mayhem. Symbols of the "dark powers" can be found almost everywhere—as Colgate-Palmolive found when the cry

was raised that their moon and stars symbol was a secret signpost for Satanists. In this millennial context the dedicated zealots have been quick to discern a bold increase in Satanic activity, examining popular culture for evidence of Satanic propaganda, and finding it in everything from cartoon characters to heavy metal music (especially when played backwards).

The views of extremists on such matters are generally dismissed by society at large. Not all of their claims, however,

Left: *King Faria, an 80-year old water-witch from San Rafael, California, averaged five requests a day from people wanting to find water on their land during Marin County's 1977 drought.*

Below: *Alexander Yeromin, a Russian faith healer. Communism's response to religion and the occult bore the hallmarks of witch-hunting.*

Above: *British women—bizarrely accused by some opponents of witchcraft—protest US Cruise missiles at Greenham Common air base in 1983. Here they carry mirrors to symbolically "turn the base inside out."*

Opposite: *Mrs. Vera Stringer cleans up after a pyromaniacal poltergeist; professional ghost-sleuths Gordon Hoener and Philip Goodwilling.*

are so frivolous; some of the issues closest to their hearts are inherently difficult, and will always remain so. In the context of Salem's witch-hunts, as we have seen, men and women were sent to the gallows on the strength of "spectral" evidence. Today, we still face the problem of determining standards of evidence for crimes in which "objective" and "scientific" criteria may not be available. Investigations of Satanic ritual abuse frequently yield evidence in the form of hysteria diagnosed as multiple personality disorder, and of memories "recovered," often many years after the event, with a therapist's help.

More difficult still to handle responsibly is the testimony of young children, which prosecutors and therapists can easily manipulate. In one recent case in the United States, a Sunday School teacher was accused by a girl of exposing himself to her. The accusation was made four months after the man had stopped teaching at the school, and at first none of the other children in the class supported the accusation. But after lengthy questioning, they testified that the teacher had done a number of bad things: he had killed a giraffe and an elephant in the classroom, had cooked monkeys, sacrificed a human baby, and forced the children to drink blood. Most of their testimony was later withdrawn, but San Diego prosecutors decided to try the case anyway, and it lasted for seven months. A jury took seven hours to find the defendant not guilty, and in 1994 the prosecution of the case was investigated by a grand jury. It found that prosecutors in the case had persuaded therapists to play the part of detectives, and warned: "When children initially say that nothing happened to them, a misguided therapist labels them as being in denial. Then 'therapy' is sometimes continued for months or years until the children disclose the answers the therapists want to hear."

On the basis of such evidence as recovered memory and children's responses to leading questions, claims have been made that organized Satanists commit many thousands of ritual murders annually in the United States. The FBI has investigated these reports, but has so far found no corroborating evidence; according to extreme accusers, this is because the Satanists dispose of the bodies in fiendishly clever ways. These exaggerated claims seem to echo the fantasies of the witchfinders of earlier times. However, disregarding the testimony of alleged victims of abuse is no solution, especially when the perpetrators of abuse crimes—ritual or otherwise—are always in a commanding position of power over their vulnerable, usually voiceless, victims.

In September, 1994, the New Hampshire Superior Court Justice William J.

THINGS THAT GO BUMP IN THE NIGHT

In January, 1920, a young boy named Alexander Urquhart lay dying in his home in Aberdeen, Scotland. Above his deathbed, explosive sounds shook the house, and objects in his room moved of their own accord. Or so the police said. In 1903, Mr. W.G. Grootendieck reported that stones had fallen slowly from the ceiling of his thatched house in Dortrecht, Sumatra. They hadn't penetrated the ceiling, but had seemed to materialize just beneath it, before drifting like leaves to the floor. A young servant boy, a coolie, was sleeping in the house at the time.

In the winter of 1904-5 a religious revival swept through Wales, attended by mysteries. In a Portmadoc butcher's shop, objects flew through the air. The police were called in, and a young girl confessed. At the home of a Mr. Howell, in Lampeter, there were strange knockings; crowds gathered on the street, and the police were called in to control them. The Bishop of Swansea investigated, but had no explanation: there were children, but they confessed nothing. Elsewhere in Wales strange lights were seen in the sky, often hovering over chapels. Perhaps they were luminous bats, or high-flying will-o'-the-wisps, which were very common in those times of fervor.

For Mrs. Vera Stringer and her young son Steven (pictured here), the fire-setting poltergeist she called Larry appeared in her home as a gray, shifting pillar of light. It burned Steven's teddy bear.

In the summer of 1919, water, gasoline, paraffin, sandalwood oil and methylated spirits began to ooze and spurt from the walls and ceilings of Swanton Novers rectory, in the English county of Norfolk. On September 2, fifty gallons of assorted liquids were caught in pans and buckets. On September 9, it was reported, a fifteen-year-old housemaid confessed: it was all a prank. A few days later she recanted: she had been threatened—had been told she had a minute to say she'd done it, or go to prison. She'd been frightened; really, she'd done nothing.

In Hydesville, New York, in 1848, there were knockings, and the bed two young girls were trying to sleep in was shaken. In Salem, young girls and adults saw things that frightened them...

When strange things happen, we may put them down to poltergeists, witchcraft, sleight of hand,

pranks, hysteria, lunacy or deceit. Still, once in a while, at night or when the wind blows, most of us wonder if something awful isn't lurking in the walls, or if something conductive isn't hidden in our bones and brains. The Haunt Hunters, above, an organization boasting over 300 members in seventeen countries, are on hand to help with emergencies.

DEMONS EXPELLED AND WELCOMED

Every culture has its own ways of coping with demons. In the West, the best-known procedure is the Christian rite of exorcism, a combative affair, for which the Roman Catholic Church's *Rituale Romanum* provides the following instructions (1947 edition, endorsed by Francis, Cardinal Spellman) :

"*Instruction # 13*: Let the priest-exorcist keep the crucifix in his hand or at least in sight. Relics of the saints, if available, should be carefully touched to the head or breast of the pos-sessed but let him beware lest these sacred objects be abused or in any way dam-aged by the devil.

Instruction # 19: When exor-cising a woman let the priest always have responsible peo-ple preferably relatives, to hold down the woman while the devil is agitating her and let him be careful not to say or do anything that might pro-voke obscene thoughts either in himself or others.

Instruction # 20: The priest should ask the devil if he was forced into the body of the possessed person by some trick of magic or an evil spell, or potion, which if the possessed has taken by mouth he should be made to vomit up. The devil must be forced to reveal any such physical evil things (potions, charms, fetishes, etc.) still outside the body, and these must be burned."

At the high point of the exorcism the following words are said:

"Most vile dragon, in the name of the immaculate lamb, who trod upon the asp and the basilisk, who conquered the lion and the dragon, I command you to get out of this man, to get out of the church of God. Tremble and flee at that name which Hell fears; that name to which the virtues of heaven, the pow-ers and dominations are subject, which the seraphim and cherubim praise with untiring voices, chanting, Holy, Holy, Holy, Lord God of Sabaoth."

A very different, in fact opposite, approach to demons is expressed in the *Chöd* ritual of Buddhist Tibet. Still widely used as a daily practice by monas-tics and lay people alike, it was devised by Machik Labdron (1031-1129). She said:

"Better than saying a hundred times, 'Protect and guard me!' is to say once, 'Eat and take my body away.' This is my Dharma tradition.
Demons arise when your mind is agitated. Mental poisons come from the percep-tion of a self.
All demons are cut through in your mind. Mind is liberated in the unborn expanse.
My tradition is to take adverse situations as the path. I teach the instructions of cutting through, asserting that unfavorable con-ditions are aids."

Thus, in this tradition, demons are welcomed because they pro-vide an opportunity for cutting through the practitioner's cling-ing to the idea of a self. In the Buddhist conception, this idea constitutes fundamental igno-rance, the failure to recognize that phenomena, being depen-dently arisen, lack (are empty of) an intrinsic nature. From such ignorance, evil and suffering arise.

Since the body is our primary reference for the idea of a self, the *Chöd* practitioner, resting in the recognition of emptiness, invites demons to come and eat his or her body: offering one's bones, flesh, and blood, one recognizes, nonetheless, that all three elements in the drama—the subject (prac-titioner), object (demons) and action (offering)— are appearances without real substance or existence.

In Tibet some people make the *Chöd* ritual their life, wandering about the country and prac-ticing in charnel grounds and other lonely and ter-rifying places. *Chöd* is also performed as a cure for those illnesses that are thought to be caused by demons, and in that case it can be performed on behalf of the sick person by an adept practitioner.

Groff evoked the cautionary sentiments of Increase Mather (see page 91) in his decision in the case of the State versus Hungerford and Moran: "The State must establish the validity of the phenomenon and process [of memory recovery] by demonstrating that the reasoning or methodology underlying the testimony is scientifically valid; and that it is capable of empirical testing and can properly be applied to the facts in issue." If victimization of the weak by the strong, in whatever form, is to be avoided, scrupulously unbiased and carefully weighed legal standards must be maintained within such emotionally charged debates.

We have seen witches in their varying cultural perspectives, from the sorceress and oracle of myth, to crones with cats and broomsticks, and learned that these portraits are often the creations of those whose power and success relied on the belief in witches—the witchfinders. We have also seen the modern practitioners

Above: *Druids celebrate the summer solstice at Stonehenge.*

Below: *English police escort young celebrants from Stonehenge on the morning of the summer solstice, 1991. They were removed to prevent damage to the monument, but many perceived the action as inspired by intolerance of their beliefs.*

Opposite: *Goblins by Goya.*

Above: *Tea-leaf reading in 1902.*

Above, right: *Puerto Rican* botanica *in New York's Spanish Harlem. Here herbal materials, charms, and religious articles are sold.*

Right: *Eggsorcism, Gypsy style.*

Opposite: *Sir Arthur Conan Doyle was convinced that young Frances Griffiths and her sister had clairvoyant access to the fairy world. It was not so, the fairy-seer later admitted: the fairies were simply cut out of a book, propped up in front of her, and photographed.*

who have defined themselves, in a large measure, by those icons of the past, and in doing so, preserve the myths and expose themselves to society's potential persecution.

History has never produced documented "proof" of witches' powers, whether for good or evil, nor has it refuted them. But history does provide a catalog of injustice, prejudice and brutality, performed for a variety of motives in the name of "the safety of the state."

A recent literary example of how new witchfinders might evolve is Margaret Atwood's novel *The Handmaid's Tale* (1986). Set in a future, war-ravaged state in which most surviving women are infertile as a result of the enemy weapons, the story portrays a regime brutally repressive to women in its determination to re-populate. The authorities employ religio-political telecasts to justify to the men their total suspension of women's freedom, while their tactics to enforce compliance among women are a combination of incarceration, secret police methods, physical humiliation and brainwashing, in the form of com-

pulsory chants, prayers, therapy and "re-education."

Fiction? Yes. Impossible? Less so than being in two places at once, the basis of "spectral" evidence. The delicate balance between the protection of the public good and of freedom of speech, conscience and worship is the controversial arena within which witchcraft, and society's perceptions of, and responses to it, lie. If and when we let the balance tilt, we face the ultimate danger of embracing the witchfinder's cruelty, and stumble backwards to unreason.

RAISING FAIRIES

The following is an article by W.B. Yeats from the first issue of the *Irish Theosophist,* (Magazine of the Dublin Theosophical Society) October 1892. Yeats never formally joined the Dublin Theosophical Society. The signature D.E.D.I. was his handle in the Order of the Golden Dawn, which he joined in 1890 after being expelled from the esoteric section of the Theosophical Society. They stand for "*Demon Est Deus Inversus*" ("A demon is an inverted god"). His companion D.D. may have been the actress Florence Farr or Maud Gonne, the Irish Nationalist.

"The occultist and student of Alchemy whom I shall call D.D. sat at opposite sides of the fire one morning, wearied with symbolism and magic. D.D. had put down a kettle to boil. We were accustomed to meet every now and then, that we might summon the invisible powers and gaze into the astral light; for we had learned to see with the internal eyes. But this morning we knew not what to summon, for we had already on other mornings invoked that personal vision of imper-

sonal good which men name Heaven, and that personal vision of impersonal evil, which men name Hell. 'We have seen the great and they have tried us,' I said. 'Let us call the little for a change. The Irish fairies may be worth seeing. There is time for them to come and go before the water is boiled.'

I used a lunar invocation and left the seeing mainly to D.D.. She saw first a thin cloud as though with the ordinary eyes and then with the interior sight, a barren mountain crest with one ragged tree. The leaves and branches of the tree were all upon one side, as though it had been blighted by the sea winds. The Moon shone through the branches and a white woman stood beneath them. We commanded this woman to show us the fairies of Ireland, marshalled in order. Immediately a great multitude of little creatures appeared, with green hair like seaweed and after them another multitude dragging a car containing an enormous bubble. The white

woman, who appeared to be their queen, said the first were the water fairies and the second the fairies of the air. They passed on and a troop who were like living flames followed and after them a singular multitude whose bodies were like the stems of flowers and their dresses like the petals. These latter fairies, after a while, stood under a green bush from which dropped honey like dew and thrust out their tongues, which were so long, that they were able to lick the honey-covered ground without stooping. These two troops were the fairies of the fire and the fairies of the earth.

Soon a great abyss appeared and in the midst was a fat serpent, with forms, half human, half animal, polishing his heavy scales. The name of this serpent was Grew-grew, and he was the chief of the wicked goblins. About him moved quantities of things like pigs, only with shorter legs, and above him in the air flew vast flocks of cherubs and bats.

Presently the bats and cherubs and the forms that had been polishing the scales of Grew-grew, rushed high up into the air and from an opposite direction appeared the troops of the good fairies, and the two kingdoms began a most terrible warfare. The evil fairies hurled burning darts but were unable to approach very near to the good fairies, for they seemed unable to bear the neighbourhood of pure spirits. The contest seemed to fill the whole heavens, for as far as the sight could go the clouds of embattled goblins went also. It is that contest of the minor forces of good and evil which knows no hour of peace but goes on everywhere and always. The fairies are the lesser spiritual moods of that universal mind, wherein every mood is a soul and every thought a body. Their world is very different from ours, and they can but appear in forms borrowed from our limited consciousness, but nevertheless, every form they take and every action they go through, has significance and can be read by the mind trained in the correspondence of sensuous form and supersensuous meaning."

Bibliography and Works Cited

ABERLE, David F. 1966. *THE PEYOTE RELIGION AMONG THE NAVAHO.* Aldine, Chicago.

ADAMS, Henry. 1986 (1904). *MONT ST. MICHEL & CHARTRES.* Penguin, New York.

ADLER, Margot. 1979. *DRAWING DOWN THE MOON: Witches, Druids, Goddess Worshippers, and Other Pagans in America Today.* Beacon Pr., Boston.

ANKARLOO, Bengt & HENNINGSEN, Gustav, eds. 1990. *EARLY MODERN EUROPEAN WITCHCRAFT.* Oxford.

BARING-GOULD, Sabine. 1968. *FREAKS OF FANATICISM & Other Strange Events.* Repr. of 1891. Singing Tree Pr., Detroit.

BARSTOW, Anne Llewellyn. 1994. *WITCHCRAZE: A New History of the European Witch Hunts. Our Legacy of Violence Against Women.* Pandora/Harper Collins, San Francisco.

BASSET, Fletcher S. 1971. *LEGENDS & SUPERSTITIONS OF THE SEA & SAILORS In All Lands & At All Times.* Singing Tree Pr., Detroit. (Repr. of 1885 edn. By Belford, Clark, Chicago & NY).

BEATTIE, John & MIDDLETON John, eds. 1969. *SPIRIT MEDIUMSHIP & SOCIETY IN AFRICA.* Africana Pub. Co., New York.

BETTELHEIM, Bruno. 1977. *THE USES OF ENCHANTMENT: The Meaning & Importance of Fairy Tales.* Knopf, New York.

BERNDT, Ronald M. & BERNDT, Catharine H. *THE FIRST AUSTRALIANS.* Ure Smith, Sydney.

BOGUET, Henri. 1929 (1590). *AN EXAMEN OF WITCHES Drawn from Various Trials of Many of this Sect in the District of Saint Oyan de Joux Commonly Known as Saint Claude in the County of Burgundy Including the Procedure Necessary to Judge in Trials for Witchcraft. (Discours des Sorciers).* Trans. E.A. Ashwin, ed. Montague Summers. John Rodker, London (repr. Barnes & Noble NY) (© 1971 Marianne Rodker).

BOVET, Richard. 1684. *Pandaemonium or The Devils Cloyster.* The Hand & Flower Pr. Aldington, Kent. 1951.

BOYER, Paul & NISSENBAUM, Stephen. 1974. *SALEM POSSESSED.* Harvard Univ. Pr., Cambridge, MA.

BRACKERT, Helmut & VOLKMAR, Sander, eds. 1985. *JACOB & WILHELM GRIMM & OTHERS: GERMAN FAIRY TALES.* Continuum, New York.

BULFINCH, Thomas. 1978. *BULFINCH'S MYTHOLOGY.* Avenel, NJ.

BURR, George Lincoln, ed. 1946. *NARRATIVES OF THE WITCHCRAFT CASES 1648-1706.* Barnes & Noble, New York.

CAMPBELL, Joseph. 1962. *THE MASKS OF GODS VOL. 2: ORIENTAL MYTHOLOGY.* Viking, New York.

CARPENTER, Thomas H. 1986, *DIONYSIAN IMAGERY IN ARCHAIC GREEK ART: ITS DEVELOPMENT IN BLACK FIGURE VASE PAINTING.* Clarendon Pr., Oxford.

CAVENDISH, Richard. 1977. *A HISTORY OF MAGIC.* Tapplinger, NY.

CLARKSON, Rosetta E. 1940. *GREEN ENCHANTMENT: The Magic Spell of Gardens.* MacMillan. (Repr. as *The Golden Age of Herbs & Herbalists,* Dover 1972).

COHN, Norman. 1975. *EUROPE'S INNER DEMONS: An Inquiry Inspired by the Great Witch-Hunt.* New York.

COLTON, Harold S. 1949. *HOPI KACHINA DOLLS With a Key to their Identification.* Univ. of New Mexico, Albuquerque.

COULTON, G.G. 1954. *LIFE IN THE MIDDLE AGES.* Cambridge Univ. Pr.

CRAWFORD, J.S. 1967. *WITCHCRAFT & SORCERY IN RHODESIA.* Internat. African Inst./Oxford Univ. Press, Oxford.

DODDS, E.R. 1968. *THE GREEKS AND THE IRRATIONAL.* Univ. Calif., Berkeley, CA.

DOUGLAS, Mary. 1970. *WITCHCRAFT CONFESSIONS & ACCUSATIONS.* Assoc. of Social Anthropologists of the Commonwealth. Tavistock, London.

DOYLE, Sir Arthur Conan. 1921. *THE WANDERINGS OF A SPIRITUALIST.* Hodder & Stoughton, London.

DRAKE, Samuel G. 1869 (1967). *ANNALS OF WITCHCRAFT IN NEW ENGLAND & Elsewhere in the United States from their First Settlement.* Benjamin Blom., New York. (1967)

EBON, Martin. 1968. *PROPHECY IN OUR TIME* New American Library, NY.

EDSALL, F.S. 1958. *THE WORLD OF PSYCHIC PHENOMENA.* David MacKay.

EISLER, Robert. [N.D.] *MAN INTO BEAST. An Anthropological Interpretation of Sadism, Masochism, & Lycanthropy.* Spring Books, London.

ELLIS, Keith. 1973. *PREDICTION AND PROPHECY.* Wayland (London).

THE ENCYCLOPEDIA OF UFOS. Ed. Ronald Story. Dolphin Books/Doubleday. Garden City, NY

EVANS, Christopher. 1974. *CULTS OF UNREASON.* Farrar, Straus & Giroux, NY.

EVANS-PRITCHARD, E.E. 1976. *WITCHCRAFT, ORACLES & MAGIC AMONG THE AZANDE.* (Abridged). Clarendon Pr., Oxford.

FOLKLORE, MYTHS & LEGENDS OF BRITAIN. Reader's Digest Assn. Ltd, London.

FORT, Charles. 1974. *THE COMPLETE BOOKS OF CHARLES FORT.* Dover, NY.

FORTUNE, R.F. 1932. *THE SORCERERS OF DOBU: The Social Anthropology of the Dobu Islanders of the Western Pacific.* E.P Dutton, NY.

FOX, Sanford J. 1968. *SCIENCE & JUSTICE: The Massachusetts Witchcraft Trials.* Johns Hopkins Univ.Pr., Baltimore.

FRAZER, Sir James George. 1963. *THE GOLDEN BOUGH. A Study in Magic & Religion.* Abridged ed. Macmillan, New York.

GARRISON, Omar. 1978. *THE ENCYCLOPAEDIA OF PROPHECY.* Citadel, Secaucus, NJ.

GINZBURG, Carlo. 1991. *ECSTASIES: Deciphering the Witches' Sabbath.* Trans. Raymond Rosenthal © Random House, 1991. Pantheon, NY. (Originally: *Storia Notturna,* Giulio Einaudi Editore, Turin, 1989).

GIVRY, Grillot de. N.D. *WITCHCRAFT, MAGIC & ALCHEMY.* Trans. J. Courtenay Locke. Bonanza, New York.

GRANT, Michael. 1982. *EROS IN POMPEII.* Bonanza, New York (Mondadori, Milan 1974).

GRAVES, Robert. 1960. *THE GREEK MYTHS.* 2 vols. Penguin, New York.

———— & PATAI, Raphael. 1966. *HEBREW MYTHS: The Book of Genesis.* McGraw-Hill, New York.

GRIMM Brothers: 1981. *THE GERMAN LEGENDS OF THE BROTHERS GRIMM.* 2 vols.; trans. & ed. Donald Ward. ISHI, Philadelphia.

GREGOR, Arthur S. 1972. *WITCHCRAFT & MAGIC: The Supernatural World of Primitive Man.* Scribner's, New York.

GUAZZO, Francesco Maria. 1929 (1608, 1626). *COMPENDIUM MALEFICARUM, Showing the Iniquitous & Execrable Operations of Witches Against the Human Race, & the Divine Remedies by which they May be Frustrated.* Trans. E.A. Ashwin, ed. Montague Summers. John Rodker, London.

HALLIDAY, W.R. 1967 (1913 repr.) *GREEK DIVINATION.* Argonaut Inc., Chicago.

HALSELL, Grace 1986. *PROPHECY AND POLITICS.* Lawrence Hill & Co.,Westport, CT.

HAMILTON, Edith. 1969. *MYTHOLOGY: Timeless Tales of Gods & Heroes.* Signet, NY.

HANSEN, Chadwick. 1969. *WITCHCRAFT AT SALEM.* Braziller, New York.

HARRISON, G.B., ed. 1929. *THE TRIAL OF THE LANCASTER WITCHES.* Peter Davies, London; facsim. edn., Barnes & Noble, New York, 1970.

HARTMAN, Marianne & HARRISON, J.K. 1982. "Health Beliefs & Realities in the Middle Income Anglo-American Neighborhood." *Advance in Nursing Practice* April, 49-64.

HEBREW BIBLE. 1963. Jewish Publication Soc. of Am., Philadelphia.

HERSKOVITS, Melville J. 1937. *LIFE IN A HAITIAN VALLEY.* Knopf, New York.

HILL, Christopher. 1984 *THE WORLD TURNED UPSIDE DOWN: Radical Ideas During the English Revolution.* Peregrine/Penguin, Harmondsworth, Mdx., England.

HILL, Douglas & WILLIAMS, Pat. 1966. *THE SUPERNATURAL.*

Hawthorn Books, New York.

HOYT, Charles Alva. 1989. *WITCHCRAFT.* Southern Illinois Univ. Pr., Carbondale & Edwardsville, IL.

JAYNES, Julian. 1976. *THE ORIGINS OF CONSCIOUSNESS IN THE BREAKDOWN OF THE BICAMERAL MIND.* Houghton Mifflin, New York.

KARLSEN, Carol F. 1987. *THE DEVIL IN THE SHAPE OF A WOMAN: Witchcraft in Colonial New England.* W.W. Norton, London & New York.

KERR, Howard & CROW, Charles L., eds 1983. *THE OCCULT IN AMERICA: New Historical Perspectives.* Univ. of Illinois Press, Urbana & Chicago.

KLUCKHORN, Clyde & LEIGHTON, Dorothea. 1951. *THE NAVAHO.* Harvard Univ. Pr., Cambridge, MA.

KRAMER, S.N. 1961. *HISTORY BEGINS AT SUMER.* Thames & Hudson, London.

LEA, H.C. 1957. *MATERIALS TOWARD A HISTORY OF WITCHCRAFT.* 3 vols. arranged & ed. Arthur C. Howland. Thomas Yoseloff, New York & London.

LHALUNGPA, Lobsang. 1977. *THE LIFE OF MILAREPA.* Dutton, New York.

LHURMAN, T.M. 1989. *PERSUASIONS OF THE WITCH'S CRAFT.* Harvard Univ. Pr., Cambridge, MA.

LUTHER, Martin. 1967. *WORKS,* Vol. 54: *TABLE TALK.* Trans. Theodore C. Tappert. Fortress.

MABINOGION, THE. 1976. Trans. Jeffrey Gantz. Penguin, New York.

MABBERLEY, D.J. 1987. *THE PLANT BOOK. A Portable Dictionary of the Higher Plants.* Cambridge Univ. Pr., Cambridge. MA.

MAPPEN, Marc, ed. 1980. *WITCHES & HISTORIANS. Interpretations of Salem.* Robert F. Krieger Pub. Co., Huntington, NY.

MARSHALL, Richard. 1993. *STRANGE, AMAZING & MYSTERIOUS PLACES.* Collins Publishers, San Francisco.

MASTERS, R.E.L. 1962. *EROS & EVIL : The Sexual Psychopathology of Witchcraft.* Julian Pr., New York.

MATHER, Cotton. 1689. *MEMORABLE PROVIDENCES RELATING TO WITCHCRAFT & POSSESSIONS, Boston.*

————1692. *THE WONDERS OF THE INVISIBLE WORLD, Boston.*

MICHELL John & RICKARD, J.M. 1977. *PHENOMENA: A Book of Wonders.* Thames & Hudson, London.

MIDDLETON, John, ed. 1967. *MAGIC, WITCHCRAFT & CURING.* Am. Mus. Nat. Hist./ Nat. Hist. Pr., Garden City, NY.

NAUERT, Charles G., Jr. 1965. *AGRIPPA & THE CRISIS OF RENAISSANCE THOUGHT.* Univ. of Illinois Pr., Urbana, IL.

NELSON, Geoffrey K. 1969. *SPIRITUALISM & SOCIETY.* Schocken Books, New York.

NEVINS, Winfield S. 1892. *WITCHCRAFT IN SALEM VILLAGE IN 1692.* Lee & Shephard, Boston. (Repr. as *The Witches of Salem,* Longmeadow Pr., Stamford CT, 1994).

NIETZSCHE, Friedrich. 1954. *THE PHILOSOPHY OF NIETZSCHE.* Trans. Var. Modern Library/ Random House, New York.

OWEN, Alex. 1990. *THE DARKENED ROOM: Women, Power & Spiritualism in Late Victorian England.* Univ. of Pennsylvania Pr., Philadelphia.

PAUWELS, Louis, & BERGIER, Jacques. 1988. *THE MORNING OF THE MAGICIANS.* Dorset Pr., trans. Anthony Gibbs. New York. 1963. orig. *Le Matins des Magiciens,* © Editions Gallimard, Paris, 1960.

PEARSALL, Ronald. 1972. *THE TABLE-RAPPERS.* Michael Joseph, London.

PETRONIUS. 1986. *THE SATYRICON.* Trans. J.P. Sullivan. Penguin, Harmondsworth, Mdx., England.

PLATO. 1977. *TIMAEUS.* Trans. Desmond Lee. Penguin Harmondsworth Mdx., England

PODMORE, Frank. 1963. *MEDIUMS OF THE 19TH CENTURY.* (2 Vols.). University Books, New Hyde Park, NY. (repr. of Podmore 1902 *Modern Spiritualism.*)

REMY, Nicolas. 1930 (1595). *DEMONOLATRY (DEMONOLATREIA): Drawn from the Capital Trials of 900 Persons, More or Less, Who Within the Last Fifteen Years Have in Lorraine Paid the Penalty of Death for the Crime of Witchcraft.* Trans. E.A. Ashwin; ed. & int. Montague Summers. John Rodker, London.

ROBBINS, Russell Hope. 1959. *THE ENCYCLOPEDIA OF WITCH-CRAFT & DEMONOLOGY.* Crown, New York.

ROHEIM, Géza. 1972. *ANIMISM, MAGIC & THE DIVINE KING.* Internat. Universities Pr., New York.

RUSSELL, Jeffrey B. 1980. *A HISTORY OF WITCHCRAFT: Sorcerers, Heretics and Pagans.* Thames and Hudson, London.

SANDRAS, N.K. 1968. *T HE EPIC OF GILGAMESH.* 1968. Penguin, New York.

SCOT, Reginald. 1584 (1964). *THE DISCOVERIES OF WITCHCRAFT.* Univ. Southern Illinois Pr., Carbondale & Edwardsville, IL. (1964).

SIR GAWAIN & THE GREEN KNIGHT. Trans. Brian Stone. 1970. Penguin, New York.

SHAKESPEARE, William. 1993. *THE YALE SHAKESPEARE: The Complete Works.* Barnes & Noble, New York.

SKEAT, Walter William. 1900. *MALAY MAGIC: An Introduction to the Folklore & Popular Religion of the Malay Peninsula.* Frank Cass & Co., London.

SISKIN, Edgar E. 1983. *WASHO SHAMANS & PEYOTISTS: Religious Conflict in an American Indian Tribe.* Univ. of Utah Pr., Salt Lake City, UT.

SPINKA, Matthew. 1941. *JOHN HUS & THE CZECH REFORM.* © Univ. Chicago. Archon Books, Hamden, CT.

SPENCE, Lewis. 1960. *AN ENCYCLOPAEDIA OF OCCULTISM.* Citadel, Secaucus, NJ.

SPRENGER, Jacobus & KRAMER, Henricus. 1485. *MALLEUS MALEFICARUM (THE HAMMER OF WITCHES which destroyeth witches & their heresy as with a two-edged sword).* Trans. Montague Summers. Benjamin Blom, New York. 1928.

STARKEY, Marion. 1969. *THE DEVIL IN MASSACHUSETTS.* Anchor Books, Garden City, NY.

STODOLA, Jirí & VOLÁK, Jan. 1994. *THE ILLUSTRATED ENCYCLOPEDIA OF HERBS: Their Medicinal & Culinary Uses.* Barnes & Noble, New York.

SUMMERS, Montague. 1926. *THE HISTORY OF WITCHCRAFT & DEMONOLOGY.* 2nd edn. (1956). University Books, New Hyde Park, NY.

————. 1927. *THE GEOGRAPHY OF WITCHCRAFT.* University Books, Evanston, NY. (1958)

TAYLOR, W.G.L. 1933. *KATE FOX & THE FOX-TAYLOR RECORD.* G.P. Putnam's Sons, New York.

TIRYAKIAN, Edward A. *ON THE MARGIN OF THE VISIBLE: Sociology, the Esoteric, & the Occult.* John Wiley, New York.

TREVOR-ROPER, Hugh. 1968. *THE EUROPEAN WITCH-CRAZE of the Sixteenth & Seventeenth Centuries & Other Essays.* Harper Torchbooks, Harper & Row, New York.

WALKER, D.P. 1981. *UNCLEAN SPIRITS: Possession & Exorcism in France & England in the Late 16th & Early 17th Centuries.* Univ. of Pennsylvania Pr., Philadelphia.

WEBSTER, Hutton. 1948. *MAGIC: A Sociological Study.* Stanford Univ. Pr., Stanford, CA.

WEISMAN, Richard. 1984. *WITCHCRAFT, MAGIC & RELIGION IN 17th-CENTURY MASSACHUSETTS.* Univ. Mass. Pr., Amherst, MA.

WEYER, Johan. 1991 (1583). *DE PRAESTIGIIS DAEMONUM (Demonic Illusions).* Trans. John Shea, ed George Mora. Medieval & Renaissance Texts & Studies: Witches, Devils & Doctors in the Renaissance. Center for Medieval & Early Renaissance Studies, State Univ. NY, Binghamton.

WIND, Edgar. 1968. *PAGAN MYSTERIES OF THE RENAISSANCE: An exploration of the philosophical & mystical sources of iconography in Renaissance art.* Norton, New York.

WILSON, Colin. 1973. *THE OCCULT.* Vintage Books/Random House, NY.

————. 1978. *MYSTERIES. An investigation into the occult, the paranormal & the supernatural.* G.P Putnam's Sons, New York.

WORDSWORTH, William. 1888. *COMPLETE POETICAL WORKS.* Macmillan, London.

YATES, Frances. 1964 *GIORDANO BRUNO & THE HERMETIC TRADITION.* Routledge & Kegan Paul/Univ. Chicago Pr., Chicago.

Index

Acknowledgements

The author would like to thank the following individuals for their kindness and diverse expertise: Joan Baumbach, Elizabeth M. Callahan, Joseph L. Halbach, Diana Hartell, Douglas W. Kinney, George Marsden, Christine Monahan-Stahl, Susan R. Parker, Mario Schittini Pinto, Sherab Posel, Larry J. Rosner, Mildred Rosner, Dennis Stahl, Lorene Weidman, and Brian Weidman.

The publisher would like to thank Nancy Carter, Claire Gordon, Emily Head, Maureen Hunt, Alain Levy, and Robin Langley Sommer for their assistance in the preparation of this book; and the following agencies and individuals for supplying illustrations:

AKG, LONDON: pages 6, 37 (both), 52, 57 (top), 70, 82, 13
THE BETTMANN ARCHIVE: 7, 8, 9, 10, 11 (both), 12, 14, 15 (both), 16, 17, 18, 19, 20, 22, 23 (both), 24 (both), 26 (both), 27, 28 (top right), 30, 31(both), 32 (both), 33 (both), 34, 36, 38, 43, 45 (both), 48, 50, 51, 53 (bottom right), 55, 56 (right), 57 (bottom), 58, 60 (top), 61, 64, 65, 66 (top), 67, 69, 71, 77, 78, 83, 84, 86, 87, 88, 90, 92, 94 (both), 96, 101 (both), 103, (bottom), 106, (top), 111 (bottom), 113, 115, 119, 121 (both), 122, 123 (right), 124, 126, 127 (both), 128, 129 (bottom), 137, 146, 147 (top), 152
BIBLIOTHÈQUE NATIONALE DE PARIS: 56 (left), 68, 106 (bottom)
GIRAUDON/ART RESOURCE, NY: 2

MARY EVANS PICTURE LIBRARY: 40, 42, 107, 110, 129 (top), 130, 132, 136, 148
METROPOLITAN MUSEUM OF ART, Fletcher Fund, 1935: 35
NORTHWIND PICTURE ARCHIVES: 3, 79, 89 (top), 97
REUTERS/BETTMANN: 98, 99, 117 (bottom), 144, 149 (bottom), 153 (both)
UPI/BETTMANN: 100, 101 (top), 103 (top), 104, 105, 109 112, 117 (top), 125 (both), 131, 138 (bottom), 139, 140, 141, 142 (left), 143, 145 (both), 147 (bottom), 149 (top), 150, 151 (both), 154 (top right), 155
© Jack Vartoogian: 102, 111 (top)
© Charles Ziga: 114